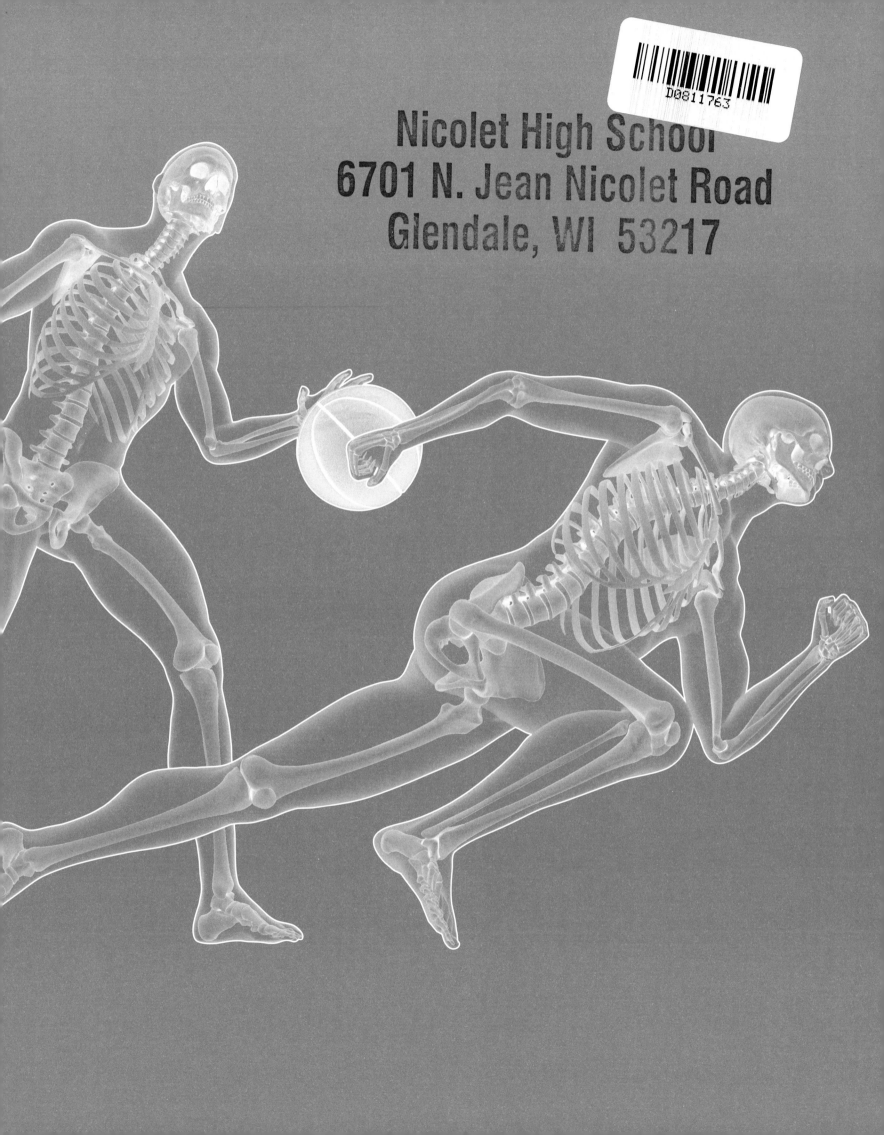

THE skeleton BOOK

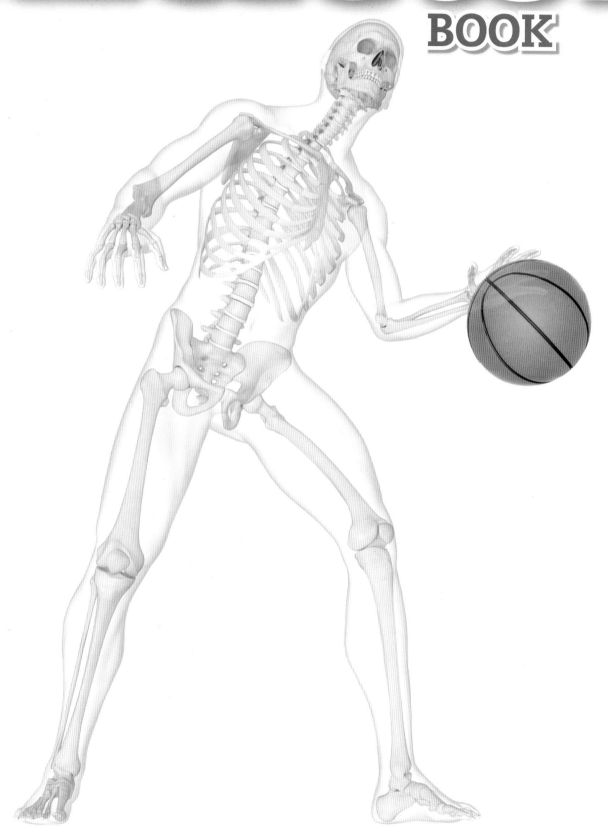

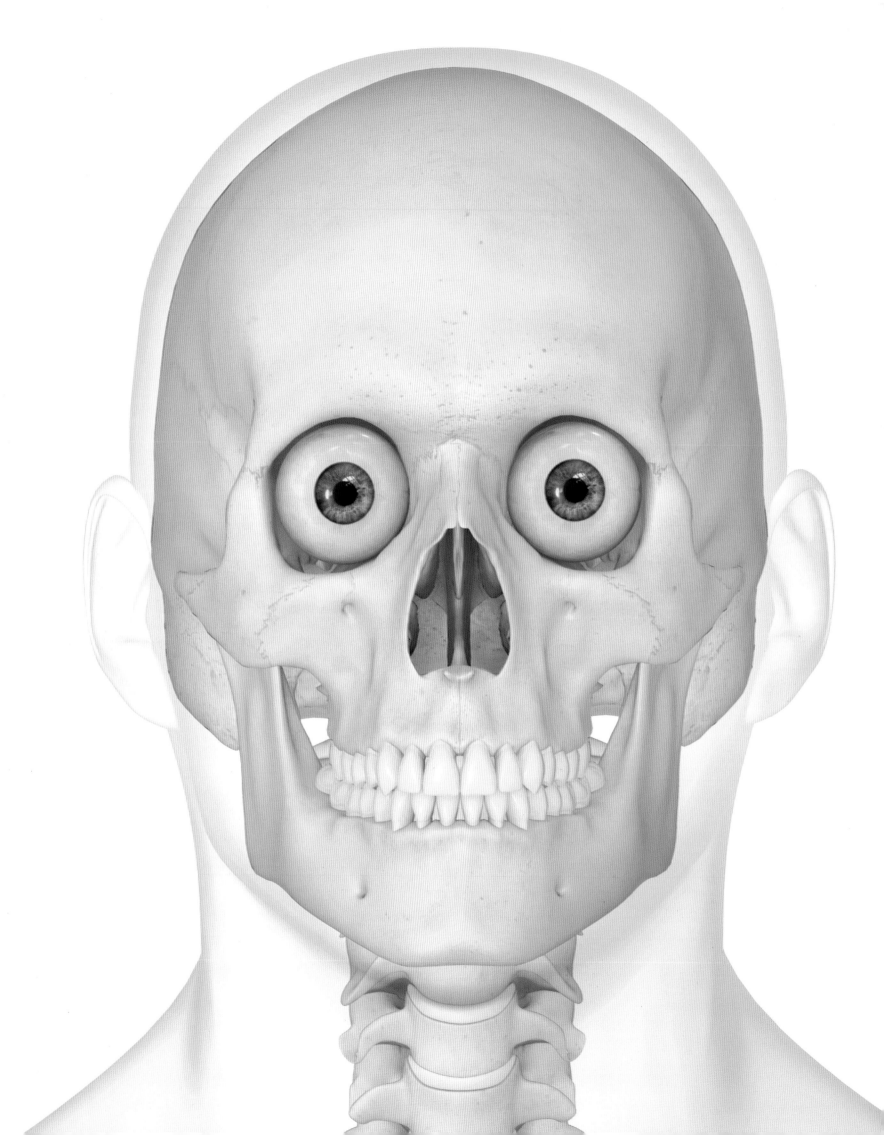

THE skeleton BOOK

CONTENTS

6 Foreword

8 Why you need a skeleton

10 Meet the family

12 Inside a bone

14 Building a skeleton

16 Growing up

18 Broken bones

20 Made to move

22 Safety helmet

24 Braincase

26 Super senses

28 Open wide

30 Growing teeth

32 Flexible neck

34 Spinal column

36 Bendable backbone

38 Shoulder support

40 Adaptable arms

42 Nimble fingers

44 Precision grip

46 Take a deep breath

48 Bony cradle

50 Swinging hips

52 Born to run

54 Longest and strongest

56 Bended knees

58 Feet first

60 On your toes

62 Bone technology

64 Bone detectives

66 Bone names

70 Glossary

72 Index

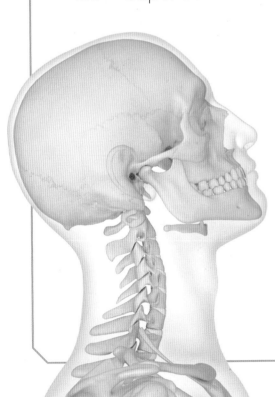

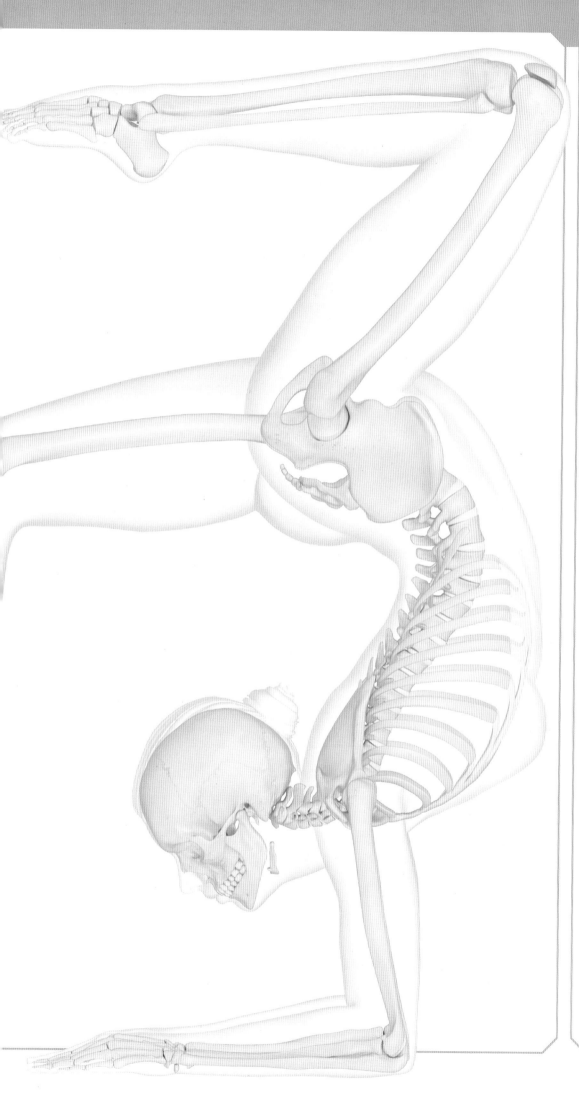

Authors Ben Morgan, Steve Parker
Consultants Professor Alice Roberts,
Dr. Kim Dennis-Bryan, Dr. Ben Garrod
Senior art editor Smiljka Surla
Senior editor Ben Morgan
Editors Shaila Brown, Steven Carton,
Ashwin Khurana
Designers Laura Gardner, Mary Sandberg,
Jacqui Swan
3D models & illustrations Arran Lewis
Illustrators Edwood Burn, Clare Joyce,
Martin@KJA-Artists.com, Michael Parkin
Managing editor Lisa Gillespie
Managing art editor Owen Peyton Jones
Producer, pre-production Gillian Reid
Senior producer Mary Slater
Jacket editor Claire Gell
Jacket designer Suhita Dharamjit
Jacket DTP designer Harish Aggarwal
Managing jackets editor Saloni Singh
Senior jacket designer Mark Cavanagh
Jackets design development manager
Sophia MTT
Publisher Andrew Macintyre
Associate publishing director Liz Wheeler
Art director Karen Self
Design director Phil Ormerod
Publishing director Jonathan Metcalf

First American Edition, 2016
Published in the United States by DK Publishing
345 Hudson Street, New York, New York 10014

Copyright © 2016 Dorling Kindersley Limited
DK, a Division of Penguin Random House LLC
16 17 18 19 20 10 9 8 7 6 5 4 3 2 1
001–282972—Sept/2016

A catalog record for this book is available
from the Library of Congress.
ISBN: 978-1-4654-5336-5

DK books are available at special discounts when
purchased in bulk for sales promotion, premiums,
fund-raising, or educational use.
For details, contact: DK Publishing Special Markets,
345 Hudson Street, New York, New York 10014
SpecialSales@dk.com

Printed and bound in China

A WORLD OF IDEAS:
SEE ALL THERE IS TO KNOW
www.dk.com

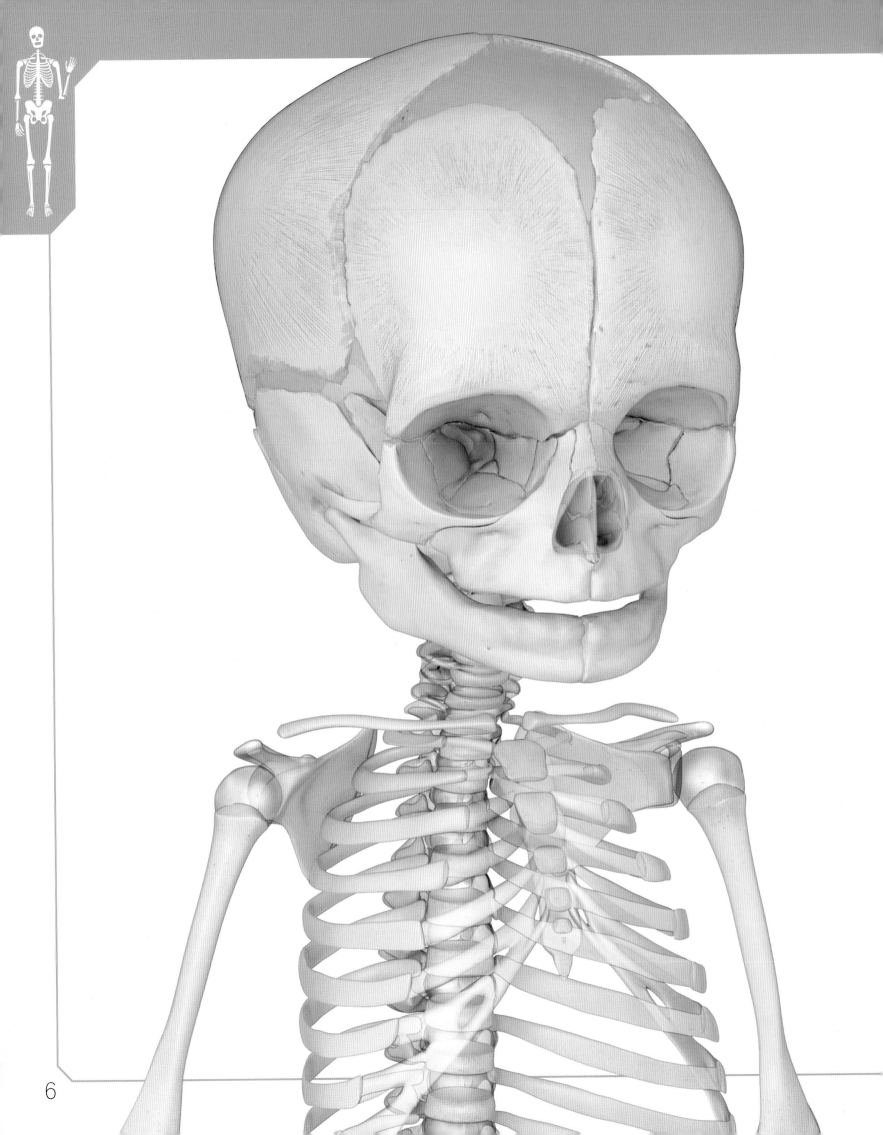

INTRODUCTION

When you see a skeleton, its strange face may seem a bit scary. But the hundreds of bones inside you are among the most extraordinary organs in your body. Evolved over millions of years, they are extremely strong, yet despite this strength, amazingly light. They are not completely rigid, though—they are flexible enough to bend just a little. If they didn't, athletes would constantly suffer broken legs.

Bones are not lifeless. They grow as you get bigger because bone-creating cells make solid minerals such as calcium phosphate and a flexible protein called collagen. If you break a bone, these cells become very active. They repair the break by making new bone and removing older, damaged bone.

We think of the skeleton as a solid scaffold that supports the body, but bones do more than that. Many of them are hollow, and the gaps inside are filled with marrow—a soft jelly that manufactures blood. It makes the red blood cells that carry oxygen around your body, the white blood cells that fight infection, and the platelets that make blood clot when you cut yourself.

The movement of the skeleton is particularly fascinating. Try extending your arm and turning your hand from left to right and back. As it twists, the small bones inside your wrist slide smoothly and silently over each other. Imagine a metal machine moving in a similar way. There might be clanking or scraping sounds, and if the movements were fast enough, the metal would get hot because of friction. But your joints make no noise or heat.

Generally our bones and joints only begin to deteriorate when we get much older. Surgeons can replace worn joints with metal ones, but no artificial knee or hip is ever as good as a natural joint. We can prevent the deterioration to some extent. A good diet and regular exercise keep bones strong—when your muscles get stronger, your bones grow thicker and stronger too.

Your skeleton is a miracle of nature and a precision instrument that no human-made machine can match. Look after it well and it will last you a lifetime.

Opposite: The skeleton two months before birth. Your skeleton starts forming eight months before you're born, and the jigsaw puzzle of your skull bones takes several years to fully merge.

WHY YOU NEED A SKELETON

Without a skeleton to hold you up and give your body shape, you'd collapse in a heap of wobbling flesh and be unable to move. Your 200 or so bones, working with over 600 muscles, form a living, mobile framework that allows you to stand, walk, jump, crouch, ride a bicycle, and write your name. Your skeleton also protects your delicate insides from harm, and the insides of the bones themselves store fat and make 200 billion new blood cells every day.

Joints between bones allow them to move, changing your body's shape.

Without a rib cage to give shape to your chest, you wouldn't be able to breathe.

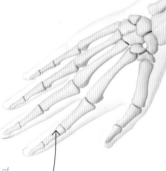

The 27 bones in each of your hands make them amazingly useful multipurpose machines.

Support

The skeleton holds up your body and gives it its shape. The main supporting column is your backbone, which carries much of your weight. It is not one bone but a stack of more than 30 interlocking bones called vertebrae.

There are about **206 bones** in the **adult skeleton** but over **300** in a **baby**. They join as the body grows.

Anchorage

Your bones serve as anchorage points for bands of tough, fibrous tissue called ligaments and tendons. Ligaments tie neighboring bones together, and tendons tie muscles to bones. When muscles contract, they pull on bones via tendons.

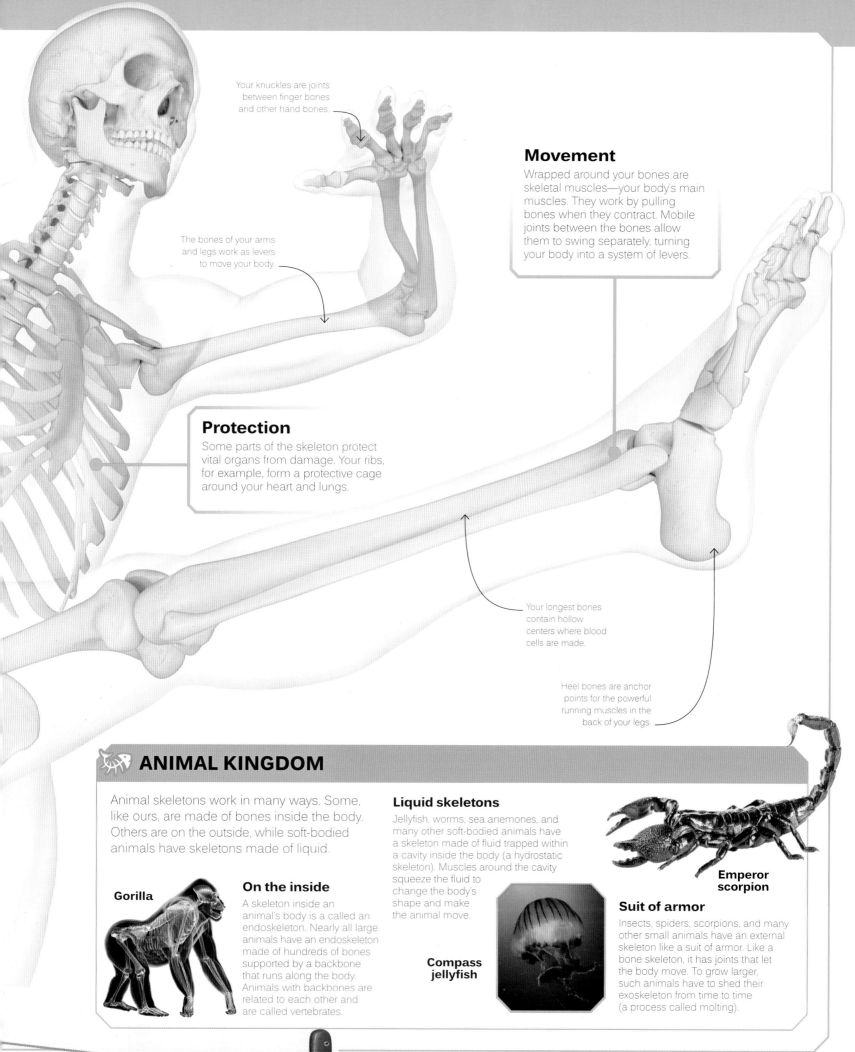

Your knuckles are joints between finger bones and other hand bones.

The bones of your arms and legs work as levers to move your body.

Movement

Wrapped around your bones are skeletal muscles—your body's main muscles. They work by pulling bones when they contract. Mobile joints between the bones allow them to swing separately, turning your body into a system of levers.

Protection

Some parts of the skeleton protect vital organs from damage. Your ribs, for example, form a protective cage around your heart and lungs.

Your longest bones contain hollow centers where blood cells are made.

Heel bones are anchor points for the powerful running muscles in the back of your legs.

ANIMAL KINGDOM

Animal skeletons work in many ways. Some, like ours, are made of bones inside the body. Others are on the outside, while soft-bodied animals have skeletons made of liquid.

Gorilla

On the inside

A skeleton inside an animal's body is a called an endoskeleton. Nearly all large animals have an endoskeleton made of hundreds of bones supported by a backbone that runs along the body. Animals with backbones are related to each other and are called vertebrates.

Liquid skeletons

Jellyfish, worms, sea anemones, and many other soft-bodied animals have a skeleton made of fluid trapped within a cavity inside the body (a hydrostatic skeleton). Muscles around the cavity squeeze the fluid to change the body's shape and make the animal move.

Compass jellyfish

Emperor scorpion

Suit of armor

Insects, spiders, scorpions, and many other small animals have an external skeleton like a suit of armor. Like a bone skeleton, it has joints that let the body move. To grow larger, such animals have to shed their exoskeleton from time to time (a process called molting).

Out of the water

One of the great steps in the history of life on Earth was the evolution of legs in vertebrates. Scientists think legs evolved in fish that used muscular fins to crawl around in shallow water. Over time, the fins got sturdier, allowing them to crawl out of the water and live on land. These were the ancestors of all land-living vertebrates alive today, including us.

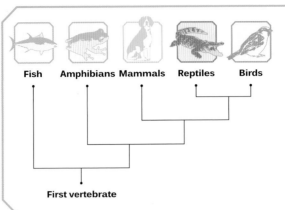

Family tree

Fish Amphibians Mammals Reptiles Birds

First vertebrate

Vertebrates are often divided into five main groups: fish, amphibians, mammals, reptiles, and birds. The family tree here shows how these are related to each other by evolution from a single common ancestor. Amphibians, mammals, reptiles, and birds make up a special group of vertebrates that all have four limbs. Scientists call them tetrapods.

MEET THE FAMILY

Our species is just one member of a family of over 64,000 animal species called vertebrates. All vertebrates have a skeleton based on the same basic plan, with a backbone of interlocking bones running through the body and a head at the front. The first vertebrates are thought to have evolved from wormlike sea creatures about 500 million years ago. Since then, evolution has reshaped their skeletons in a bewildering variety of ways, giving rise to the largest, fastest, and smartest animals ever to walk, swim, or fly on Earth.

Fish

The skeletons of fish are usually delicate because their body weight is supported by water. Most fish move by using muscles on the side of the body to flex the backbone and tail. Instead of limbs, they have fins, which are used to steer.

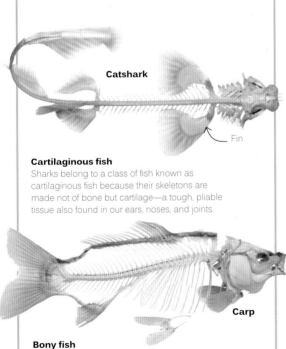

Catshark

Fin

Cartilaginous fish

Sharks belong to a class of fish known as cartilaginous fish because their skeletons are made not of bone but cartilage—a tough, pliable tissue also found in our ears, noses, and joints.

Carp

Bony fish

The vast majority of fish species have a skeleton hardened with calcium minerals to form bone. Most of these are ray-finned fish, with fins made of many slender bones.

Amphibians

Adult amphibians typically have legs and can move on land, but the young are legless, fishlike creatures that breathe with gills. Most amphibians spend part or even all of their life in water and usually lay their eggs in water.

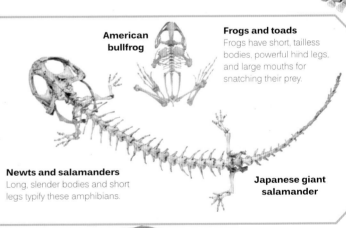

American bullfrog

Frogs and toads

Frogs have short, tailless bodies, powerful hind legs, and large mouths for snatching their prey.

Newts and salamanders

Long, slender bodies and short legs typify these amphibians.

Japanese giant salamander

Reptiles

Reptiles are better suited to life on land than amphibians. Their skeletons are shaped like those of salamanders, but reptiles have tough, scaly skin and lay eggs with protective shells that can survive out of water.

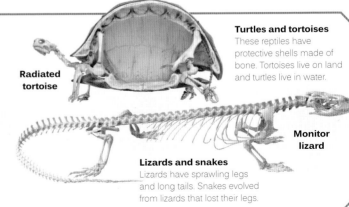

Radiated tortoise

Turtles and tortoises

These reptiles have protective shells made of bone. Tortoises live on land and turtles live in water.

Lizards and snakes

Lizards have sprawling legs and long tails. Snakes evolved from lizards that lost their legs.

Monitor lizard

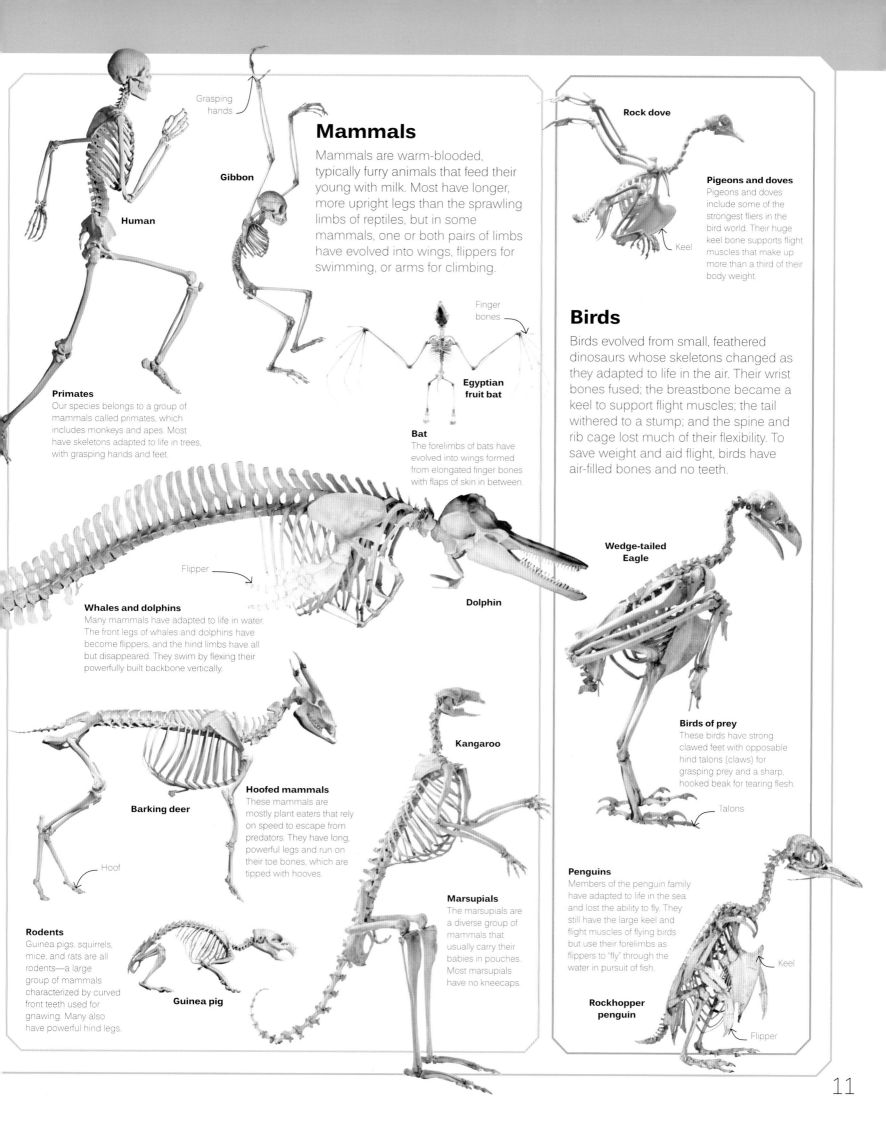

Mammals

Mammals are warm-blooded, typically furry animals that feed their young with milk. Most have longer, more upright legs than the sprawling limbs of reptiles, but in some mammals, one or both pairs of limbs have evolved into wings, flippers for swimming, or arms for climbing.

Grasping hands

Gibbon

Human

Finger bones

Egyptian fruit bat

Primates
Our species belongs to a group of mammals called primates, which includes monkeys and apes. Most have skeletons adapted to life in trees, with grasping hands and feet.

Bat
The forelimbs of bats have evolved into wings formed from elongated finger bones with flaps of skin in between.

Flipper

Whales and dolphins
Many mammals have adapted to life in water. The front legs of whales and dolphins have become flippers, and the hind limbs have all but disappeared. They swim by flexing their powerfully built backbone vertically.

Dolphin

Barking deer

Hoofed mammals
These mammals are mostly plant eaters that rely on speed to escape from predators. They have long, powerful legs and run on their toe bones, which are tipped with hooves.

Hoof

Kangaroo

Rodents
Guinea pigs, squirrels, mice, and rats are all rodents—a large group of mammals characterized by curved front teeth used for gnawing. Many also have powerful hind legs.

Guinea pig

Marsupials
The marsupials are a diverse group of mammals that usually carry their babies in pouches. Most marsupials have no kneecaps.

Birds

Birds evolved from small, feathered dinosaurs whose skeletons changed as they adapted to life in the air. Their wrist bones fused; the breastbone became a keel to support flight muscles; the tail withered to a stump; and the spine and rib cage lost much of their flexibility. To save weight and aid flight, birds have air-filled bones and no teeth.

Rock dove

Pigeons and doves
Pigeons and doves include some of the strongest fliers in the bird world. Their huge keel bone supports flight muscles that make up more than a third of their body weight.

Keel

Wedge-tailed Eagle

Birds of prey
These birds have strong clawed feet with opposable hind talons (claws) for grasping prey and a sharp, hooked beak for tearing flesh.

Talons

Penguins
Members of the penguin family have adapted to life in the sea and lost the ability to fly. They still have the large keel and flight muscles of flying birds but use their forelimbs as flippers to "fly" through the water in pursuit of fish.

Keel

Rockhopper penguin

Flipper

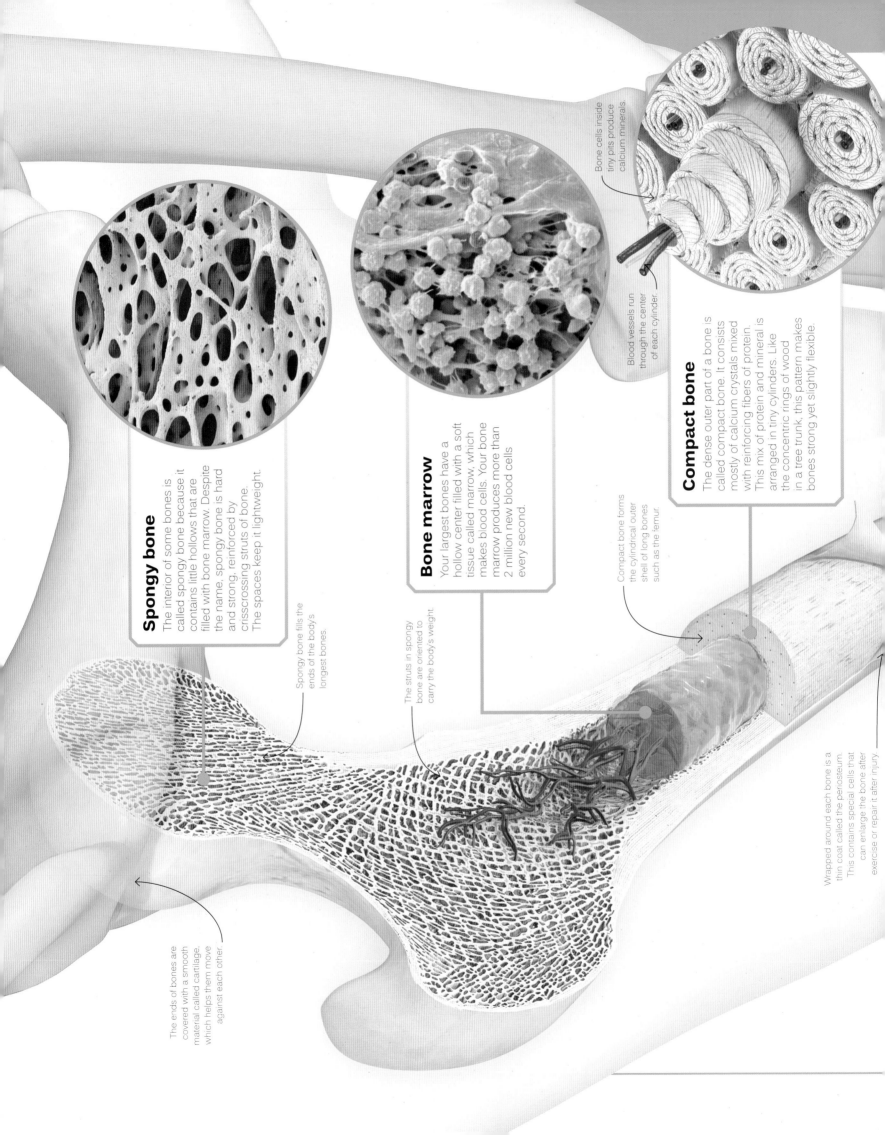

Spongy bone

The interior of some bones is called spongy bone because it contains little hollows that are filled with bone marrow. Despite the name, spongy bone is hard and strong, reinforced by crisscrossing struts of bone. The spaces keep it lightweight.

Spongy bone fills the ends of the body's longest bones.

The struts in spongy bone are oriented to carry the body's weight.

Bone marrow

Your largest bones have a hollow center filled with a soft tissue called marrow, which makes blood cells. Your bone marrow produces more than 2 million new blood cells every second.

Compact bone forms the cylindrical outer shell of long bones such as the femur.

Compact bone

The dense outer part of a bone is called compact bone. It consists mostly of calcium crystals mixed with reinforcing fibers of protein. This mix of protein and minerals is arranged in tiny cylinders. Like the concentric rings of wood in a tree trunk, this pattern makes bones strong yet slightly flexible.

Bone cells inside tiny pits produce calcium minerals.

Blood vessels run through the center of each cylinder.

The ends of the bones are covered with a smooth material called cartilage, which helps them move against each other.

Wrapped around each bone is a thin coat called the periosteum. This contains special cells that can enlarge the bone after exercise or repair it after injury.

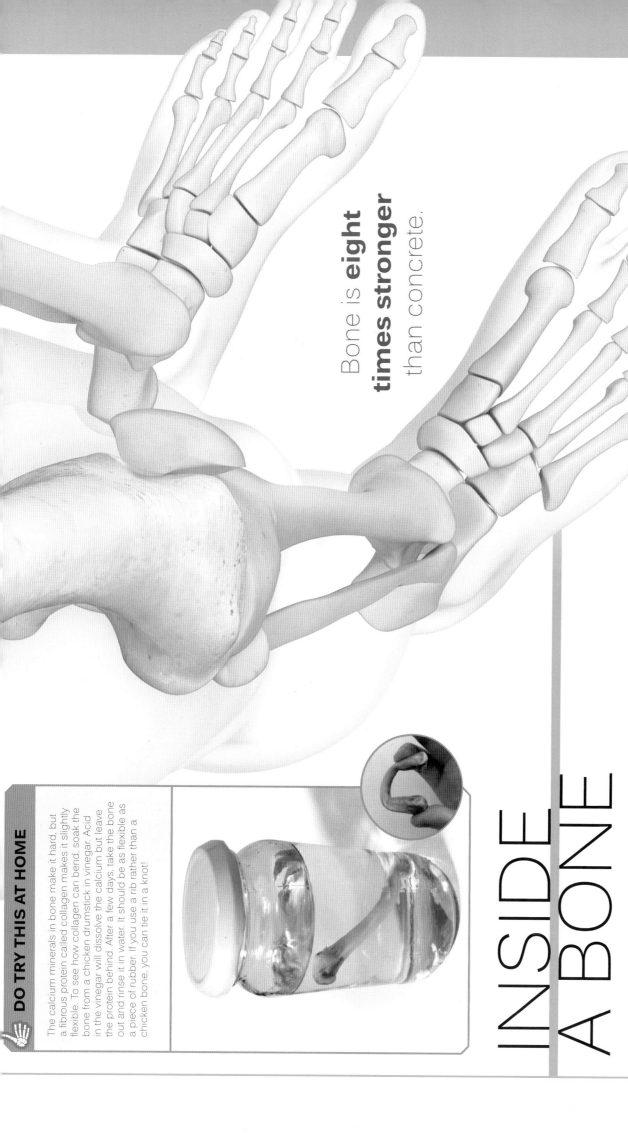

Bone is **eight times stronger** than concrete.

INSIDE A BONE

Imagine you had X-ray vision and could look inside your leg to see your thigh bone—the longest bone in your body. You'd see that although a bone looks solid from the outside, its inside is a honeycomb of spaces filled with other kinds of tissue, such as bone marrow. Only the outer layer is dense and solid, but even this contains tiny channels for blood vessels and microscopic pits in which living bone cells are trapped. Bones get their strength from crystals of calcium phosphate—the same mineral that makes your teeth hard. But unlike teeth, which are brittle, bones can bend slightly.

BUILDING A SKELETON

Your skeleton began to form about eight months before you were born, when you were no bigger than a grain of rice. At first it was made not of bone but of cartilage—the tough, rubbery material that still gives shape to your nose and ears. As your body grew inside your mother's womb, the cartilage was slowly replaced by bone—a process that continues well into your teenage years.

A baby's skull has large gaps called fontanelles between the bones. These fill in by the age of 18 months.

The skull bones are separate, allowing them to overlap when the baby's head squeezes through the mother's birth canal.

10 weeks

Most of a baby's skeleton is cartilage at ten weeks, but bone (here colored red) has begun to replace cartilage (blue) in the ribs, the jaw, and the middle of the leg and arm bones.

17 weeks

Seven weeks later, the baby's bones, joints, and muscles have matured enough for it to begin moving its body. This is when mothers first feel the baby move inside them.

30 weeks

The skeleton is complete at 30 weeks, but large parts still consist of cartilage instead of bone, including joints such as the wrists, ankles, hips, and knees. The skull and pelvis are made of separate parts that don't fuse until long after birth.

Actual size

The skull forms from a web of needle-shaped bones that slowly merge.

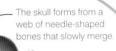

Half actual size

How hands form

Our limbs grow from tiny, paddle-shaped buds that appear when our bodies are only 0.15 in (4 mm) long. Pockets of cells at the tips of the limbs are genetically programmed to die, causing fingers and toes to form. Fingers develop first, and toes appear a few days later.

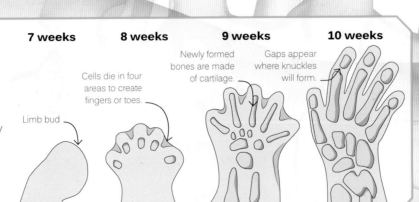

7 weeks   **8 weeks**   **9 weeks**   **10 weeks**

Cells die in four areas to create fingers or toes.

Newly formed bones are made of cartilage.

Gaps appear where knuckles will form.

Limb bud

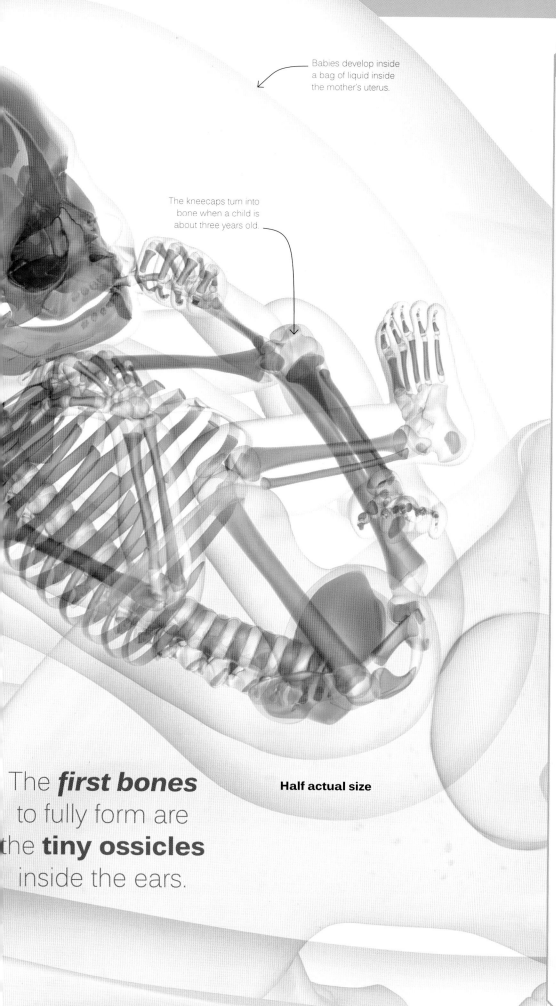

Babies develop inside a bag of liquid inside the mother's uterus.

The kneecaps turn into bone when a child is about three years old.

Half actual size

The ***first bones*** to fully form are the **tiny ossicles** inside the ears.

ANIMAL KINGDOM

All vertebrates start life in much the same way, growing from a single cell into a comma-sized speck with the beginnings of a head and backbone. As the skeleton begins to take shape, the various bones grow at different rates in different species, giving each animal the distinct body shape that suits its particular way of life.

Growing wings

Bats often develop with their wings over their faces to give the long wing bones room to grow. This bat embryo has been colored with two dyes that reveal the growing skeleton. A blue dye stains cartilage, and a red dye stains bone. Just as in a human embryo, the joints are made of cartilage.

Long-legged bat at 20 weeks

Baby rats

The jaws, spine, and arm bones of this unborn rat have turned to bone, but its hind legs and paw bones are still cartilage. Rat embryos develop quickly, spending only three weeks in the womb, but they are born helpless, furless, and blind.

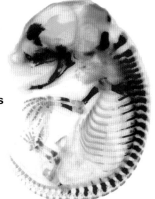

Rat at 2 weeks

Crocodile egg

Most reptiles and birds develop outside their mother's body in eggs. The shell provides a store of calcium minerals for the growing bones. Baby crocodiles spend about 12 weeks in the eggs before hatching out.

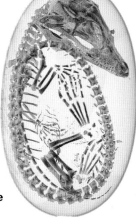

Nile crocodile at 12 weeks

GROWING UP

A baby's skeleton is not just a miniature version of an adult one. In fact, many of its "bones" are not made of bone but of cartilage—a softer tissue that can grow. Cartilage made up most of your skeleton before birth and is slowly replaced by bone cells as you get older. Throughout childhood, zones of cartilage keep actively growing at key points in your skeleton, making your bones longer and your skeleton taller. But when you reach your late teens, hormones kill these cartilage cells and your skeleton stops growing.

Growth plates

Bones grow longer thanks to special bands of cartilage called growth plates, seen here under a microscope. The dark blue layer shows rapidly dividing cartilage cells. Older cells pile up below (pale blue), making the shaft of the bone longer. The older cells then die (pink layer) and bone cells replace them.

Growth hormone

The growth of your skeleton is controlled by hormones circulating in your blood. The most important one is growth hormone, which is released by your brain and makes the growth plates in bones more active, causing bones to lengthen. In the teenage years, a surge of growth hormone triggers a growth spurt.

Robert Wadlow, the tallest man in history, was 8 ft 11 in (2.7 m) tall. An abnormally high level of growth hormone made his bones keep growing throughout his life.

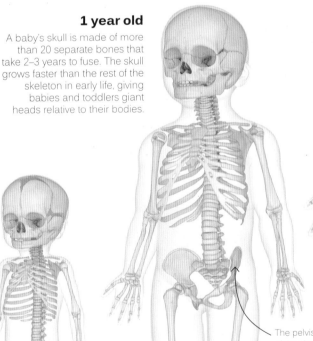

4 years old
By the age of 4, most of the cartilage has turned to bone, but there are cartilage-filled gaps near the ends of the long bones. These growth plates allow bones to grow longer.

Growth plate

1 year old
A baby's skull is made of more than 20 separate bones that take 2–3 years to fuse. The skull grows faster than the rest of the skeleton in early life, giving babies and toddlers giant heads relative to their bodies.

Growth plate

The pelvis (hip) is one of the slowest-growing parts of the skeleton, staying as six separate bones for many years.

Two months before birth
By two months before birth, much of the cartilage in a baby's body has turned to bone, but joints are still made of cartilage. Many of the bones are made of separate parts that won't fuse together until later. This is why babies have more than 300 bones but adults have only around 206.

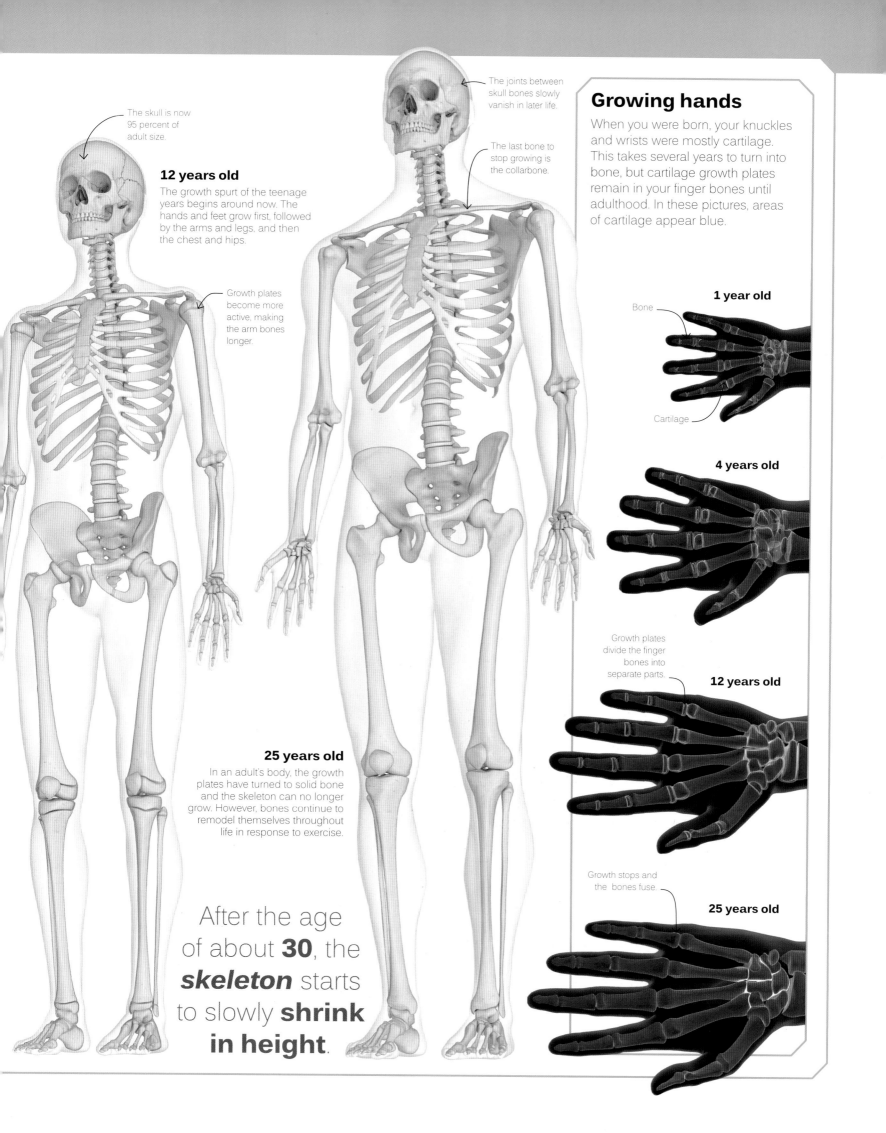

The skull is now 95 percent of adult size.

12 years old

The growth spurt of the teenage years begins around now. The hands and feet grow first, followed by the arms and legs, and then the chest and hips.

Growth plates become more active, making the arm bones longer.

The joints between skull bones slowly vanish in later life.

The last bone to stop growing is the collarbone.

Growing hands

When you were born, your knuckles and wrists were mostly cartilage. This takes several years to turn into bone, but cartilage growth plates remain in your finger bones until adulthood. In these pictures, areas of cartilage appear blue.

1 year old

Bone

Cartilage

4 years old

Growth plates divide the finger bones into separate parts.

12 years old

25 years old

In an adult's body, the growth plates have turned to solid bone and the skeleton can no longer grow. However, bones continue to remodel themselves throughout life in response to exercise.

Growth stops and the bones fuse.

25 years old

After the age of about **30**, the *skeleton* starts to slowly **shrink in height**.

BROKEN BONES

Bones are tough, but violent forces can make them crack, causing a fracture. When a bone fractures, the process of self-repair begins immediately. Special cells hidden inside every bone spring into action and multiply, bridging the gap with a makeshift repair that is later replaced by bone. It takes only a few weeks for a fracture to stabilize, but the remodeling process that restores the bone's original shape can take years to complete.

Treating fractures

Many fractures heal of their own accord, but some need a helping hand. If the fragments have moved apart, a doctor will realign them. Sometimes fractured bones have to be held in place by metal plates screwed directly into the bone. A plaster or fiberglass cast may also be worn to keep the bone still while it heals.

Metal plates hold broken bones together. They can be left in the body for life.

First hours

Within hours of a fracture, blood fills the break and forms a solid clot. Blood vessels in the area constrict, limiting further bleeding. The fracture site becomes very painful, which helps keep the bone still as it begins to heal.

Several days later

Cartilage cells multiply and replace the clot with much tougher cartilage tissue, joining the broken ends together. This forms a kind of scar called a soft callus, giving some strength back. Bone cells begin to produce new bone in the callus.

American motorcycle stuntman *Evel Knievel* had **433 fractures** in his life.

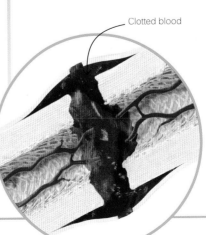

Clotted blood

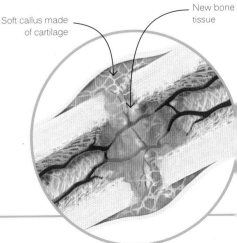

Soft callus made of cartilage

New bone tissue

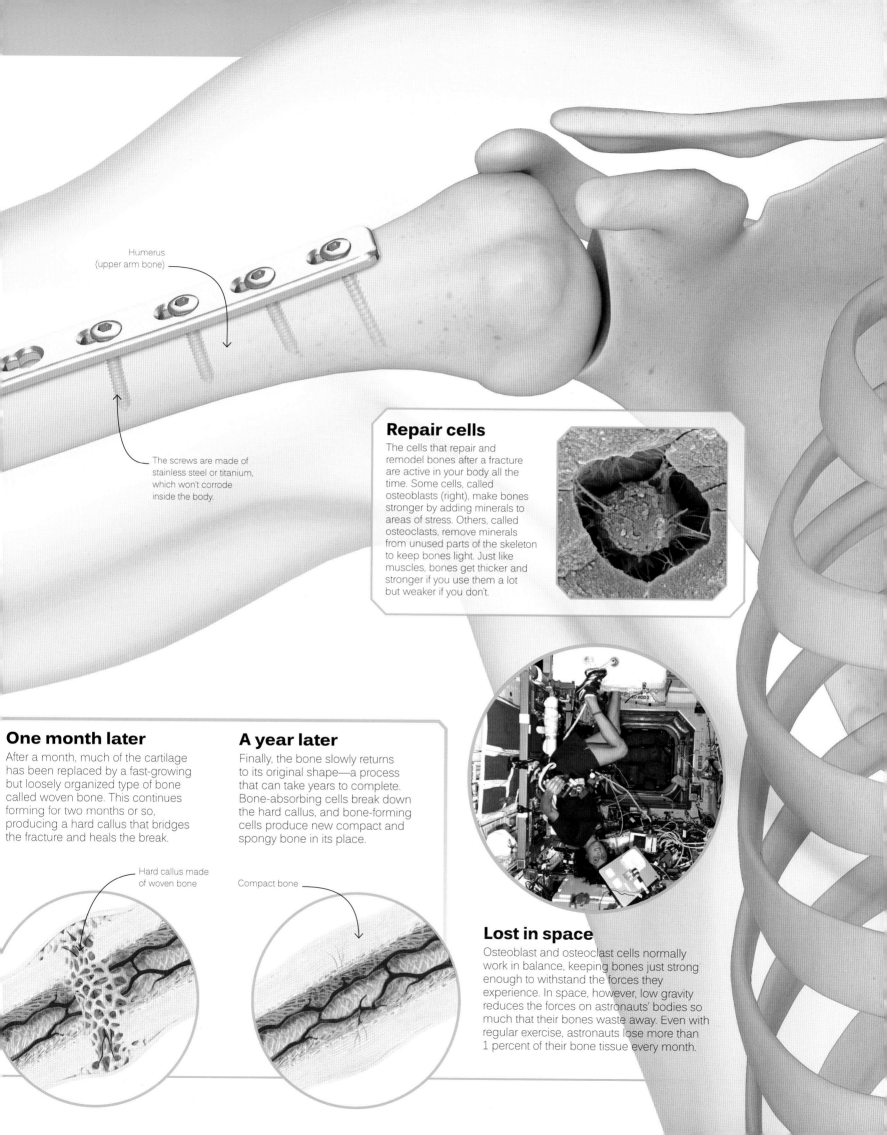

Humerus
(upper arm bone)

The screws are made of
stainless steel or titanium,
which won't corrode
inside the body.

Repair cells

The cells that repair and
remodel bones after a fracture
are active in your body all the
time. Some cells, called
osteoblasts (right), make bones
stronger by adding minerals to
areas of stress. Others, called
osteoclasts, remove minerals
from unused parts of the skeleton
to keep bones light. Just like
muscles, bones get thicker and
stronger if you use them a lot
but weaker if you don't.

One month later

After a month, much of the cartilage
has been replaced by a fast-growing
but loosely organized type of bone
called woven bone. This continues
forming for two months or so,
producing a hard callus that bridges
the fracture and heals the break.

A year later

Finally, the bone slowly returns
to its original shape—a process
that can take years to complete.
Bone-absorbing cells break down
the hard callus, and bone-forming
cells produce new compact and
spongy bone in its place.

Hard callus made
of woven bone

Compact bone

Lost in space

Osteoblast and osteoclast cells normally
work in balance, keeping bones just strong
enough to withstand the forces they
experience. In space, however, low gravity
reduces the forces on astronauts' bodies so
much that their bones waste away. Even with
regular exercise, astronauts lose more than
1 percent of their bone tissue every month.

MADE TO MOVE

Your skeleton isn't simply a rigid frame that holds you up. If it were, your body would be frozen like a statue. To let you move around, your bones are connected at flexible meeting points called joints. There are hundreds of these in your body, and many of them work like the moving parts of a machine. The joints in your elbows work like hinges, for example, and your hip joints work like the joysticks on a game controller.

Neck

Pivot joints swivel around like a steering wheel. The one at the top of your neck lets you turn your head from side to side. Try it—you should be able to turn your chin almost all the way to each shoulder. Owls' heads turn so far that they can face backward.

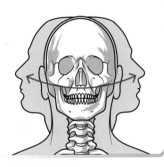

Your elbow joint locks when you fully extend an arm. This stops it from bending the wrong way.

The bones of your skull are glued together by special joints that don't allow any movement.

Shoulder

The joints in your shoulders and hips are called ball-and-socket joints because the ball-shaped end of one bone fits into a rounded socket in another. These joints let you move your arms and legs freely in any direction.

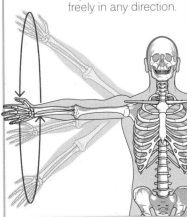

Shoulder blade

Joints between your ribs and backbone allow the ribs to swing upward when you breathe deeply.

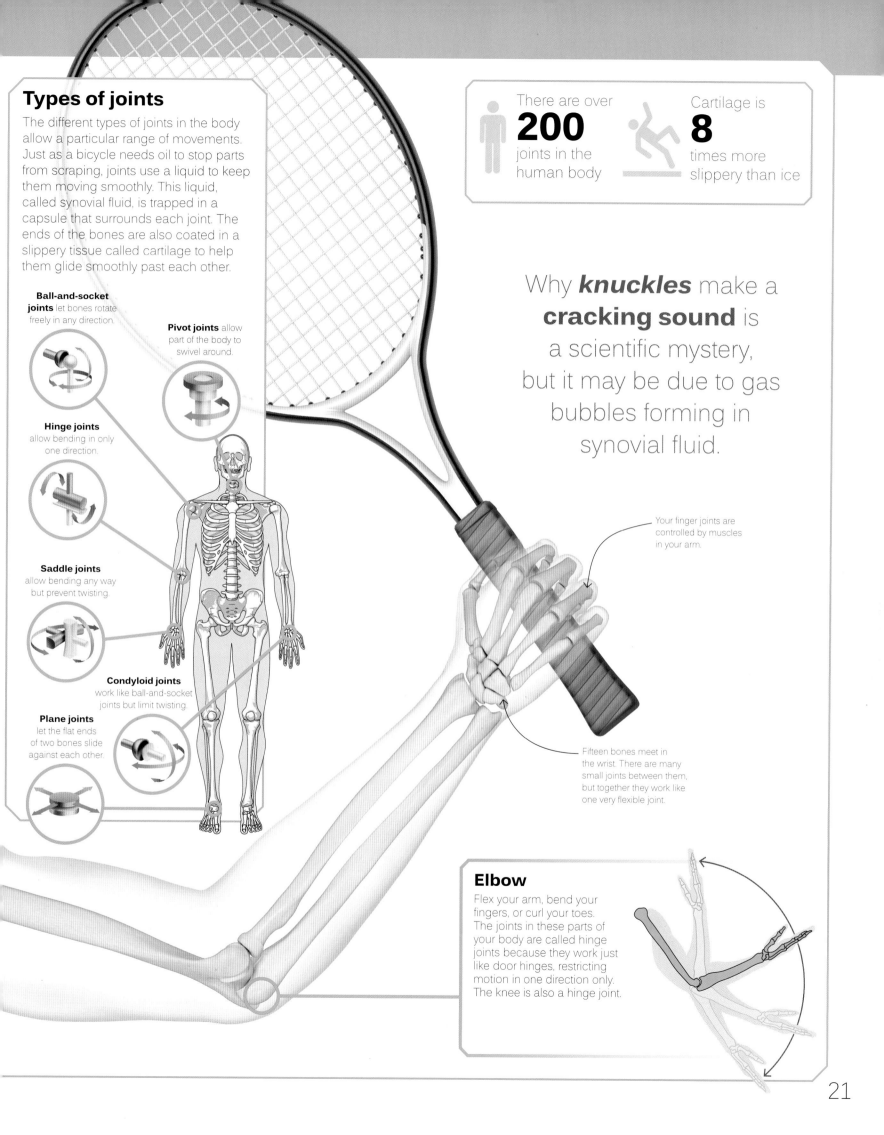

Types of joints

The different types of joints in the body allow a particular range of movements. Just as a bicycle needs oil to stop parts from scraping, joints use a liquid to keep them moving smoothly. This liquid, called synovial fluid, is trapped in a capsule that surrounds each joint. The ends of the bones are also coated in a slippery tissue called cartilage to help them glide smoothly past each other.

Ball-and-socket joints let bones rotate freely in any direction.

Pivot joints allow part of the body to swivel around.

Hinge joints allow bending in only one direction.

Saddle joints allow bending any way but prevent twisting.

Condyloid joints work like ball-and-socket joints but limit twisting.

Plane joints let the flat ends of two bones slide against each other.

There are over **200** joints in the human body

Cartilage is **8** times more slippery than ice

Why **knuckles** make a **cracking sound** is a scientific mystery, but it may be due to gas bubbles forming in synovial fluid.

Your finger joints are controlled by muscles in your arm.

Fifteen bones meet in the wrist. There are many small joints between them, but together they work like one very flexible joint.

Elbow

Flex your arm, bend your fingers, or curl your toes. The joints in these parts of your body are called hinge joints because they work just like door hinges, restricting motion in one direction only. The knee is also a hinge joint.

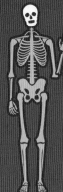

SAFETY HELMET

During your life, you'll hit your head hundreds of times—playing football, falling on the ground, bumping into furniture, and so on. To protect your fragile brain from damage, it is completely enclosed by a natural helmet of bone: your skull. The human skull is made of interlocking bones that fuse together as you grow to form a single, solid case. It isn't just a protective helmet, though—it also performs a host of other vital jobs. It allows you to eat, breathe, and speak, and it houses all your major sense organs.

The left and right parietal bones are the largest bones in the skull and form its roof.

Parietal bone

The temporal bone houses the delicate sense organs of the inner ear. They are surrounded by the hardest, densest bone in the body.

Temporal bone

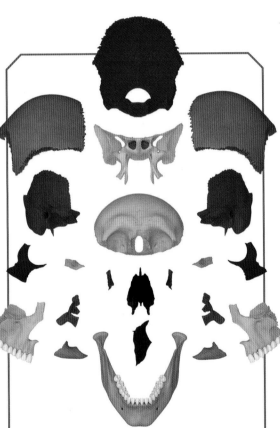

Joint

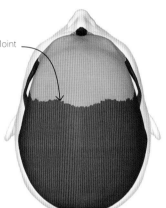

Top

The dome-shaped top of the skull is called the skullcap. It's made of large, curved bones glued rigidly together along wiggly joints called sutures. In babies, these bones are separate, which allows the head to change shape as it squeezes during birth.

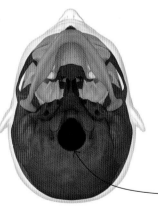

Bottom

In the base of the skull is a hole called the foramen magnum. Nerves and blood vessels pass through this, connecting the brain and body. In most animals, the hole is at the back of the skull, but humans are different. Because we stand upright, with our heads perched on top of the spine, the hole is near the middle.

Foramen magnum

Jigsaw puzzle

The skull is a three-dimensional jigsaw puzzle made of 29 bones that form separately before birth and slowly join. Many of the bones are mirrored on the left and right sides of the skull.

Back

To support the weight of the head, which makes up about 10 percent of body weight, the skull sits on the stack of bones that form the spine. Powerful muscles anchor the back of the head to the spine and shoulders.

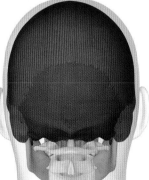

The frontal bone consists of separate left and right halves at birth, but these soon fuse to form a single bone.

Only the **top part of your nose** is made of bone—the rest is cartilage.

Frontal bone

Each eye socket is made up of seven bones.

Sphenoid bone

Ethmoid bone

Nasal bone

Zygomatic bone (cheek bone)

Maxilla (upper jaw)

Mandible (lower jaw)

Small holes in the skull allow nerves and blood vessels to pass through.

ANIMAL KINGDOM

All animal skulls do the job of protecting the brain and sense organs, but their shapes vary enormously, reflecting different lifestyles and ways of feeding.

Big-headed

The biggest skulls belong to the animals with the biggest mouths—whales. The blue whale's skull is as heavy as an adult elephant. The whale uses its giant jaws to gulp huge mouthfuls of seawater and then strain out tiny animals.

Blue whale

Head-butters

Bighorn sheep skulls are built to withstand violent blows. In the mating season, the males battle over females by slamming their heads together. Slightly loose joints help the skulls absorb the forces.

Bighorn sheep

Hole in the head

The skulls of baby monkeys and apes bear a striking similarity to human skulls. This infant monkey skull still has large gaps called fontanelles between the growing bones. These make birth easier.

Spider monkey

Armored head

Some reptiles produce bone in their scales, forming a suit of defensive armor. The armadillo lizard can also curl up into a spiky ball for extra protection.

Armadillo lizard

Trombone head

The strange curly shape on a hornbill's beak is called a casque and is made not of bone but of keratin—the same substance fingernails are made from. The casque is hollow and may help to amplify the bird's gooselike, honking calls.

Hornbill

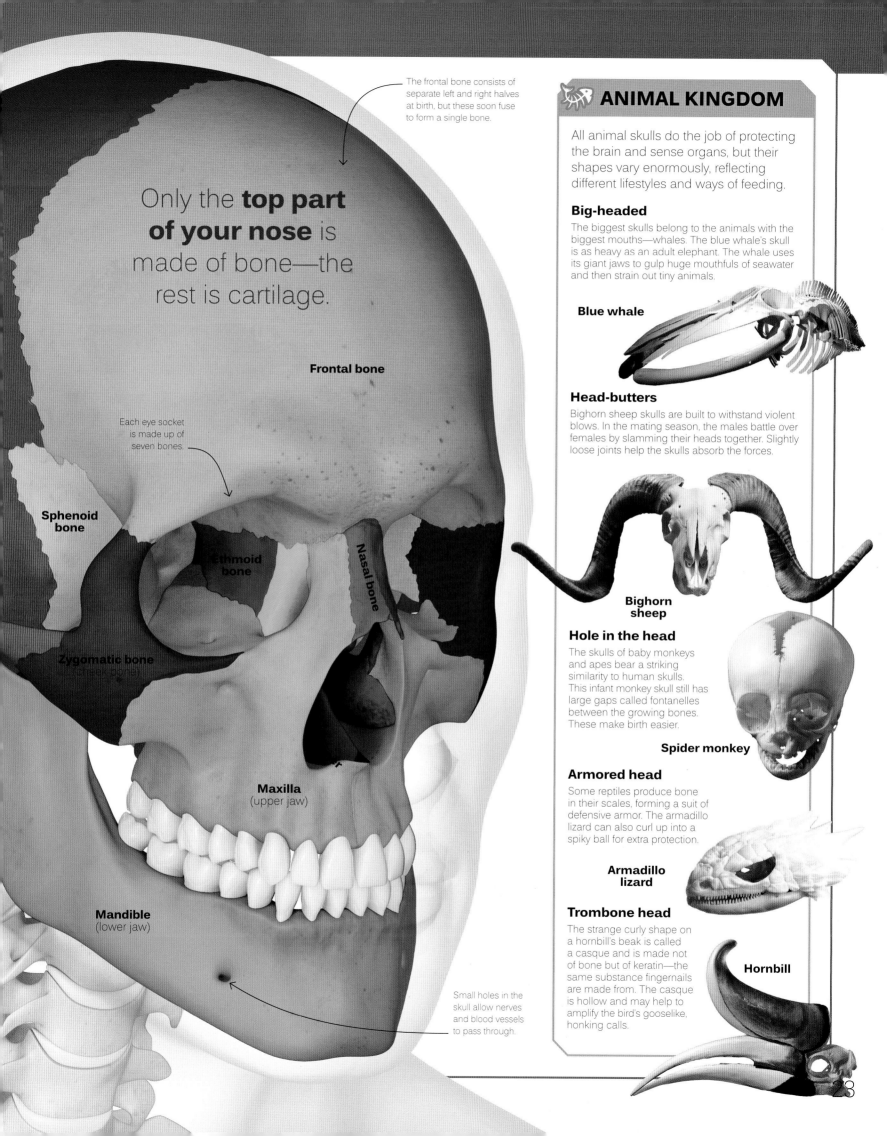

BRAINCASE

Compare a human skull to that of another mammal and you immediately notice something odd. Most mammals have a long snout with a small braincase behind it, but we have a flat face, a towering forehead, and a huge, balloonlike braincase. The reason for the difference lies in our unusual brains, which are three times larger than the brains of our closest animal relatives.

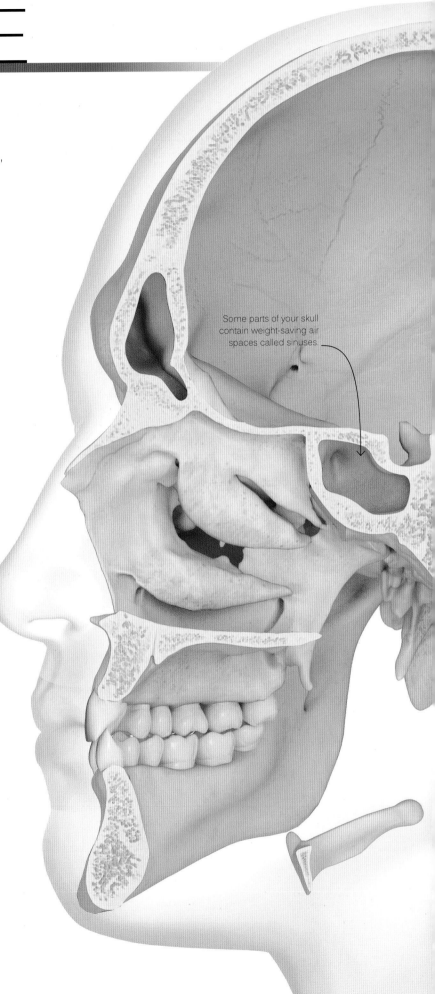

Some parts of your skull contain weight-saving air spaces called sinuses.

Ballooning brains

Fossil skulls show that our ancestors' brains went through a surge in size in the last 3 million years, tripling in volume. Some scientists think extra brainpower was needed for social reasons. Living in large groups meant that people needed to be smart to understand each other and work together. Big brains also gave our own species an ability no other animals have: complex language.

Brain size (cm³)

- 1,500
- 1,000
- 500
- 0

Australopithecus africanus — *Homo habilis* — *Homo erectus* — Neanderthals — Modern humans

4 million years ago — 2 — 0

Shrinking brains

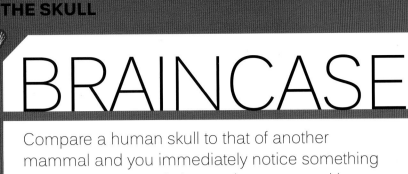

For most of history, our ancestors' brains got bigger, but in the last 20,000 years the trend reversed and brains got smaller. Even the Stone Age Neanderthals—close cousins of our own species who vanished 40,000 years ago—had brains bigger than ours. One explanation may simply be that Stone Age people were heavier and more muscular than we are, and that bigger bodies need bigger brains to control them.

Neanderthal reconstruction

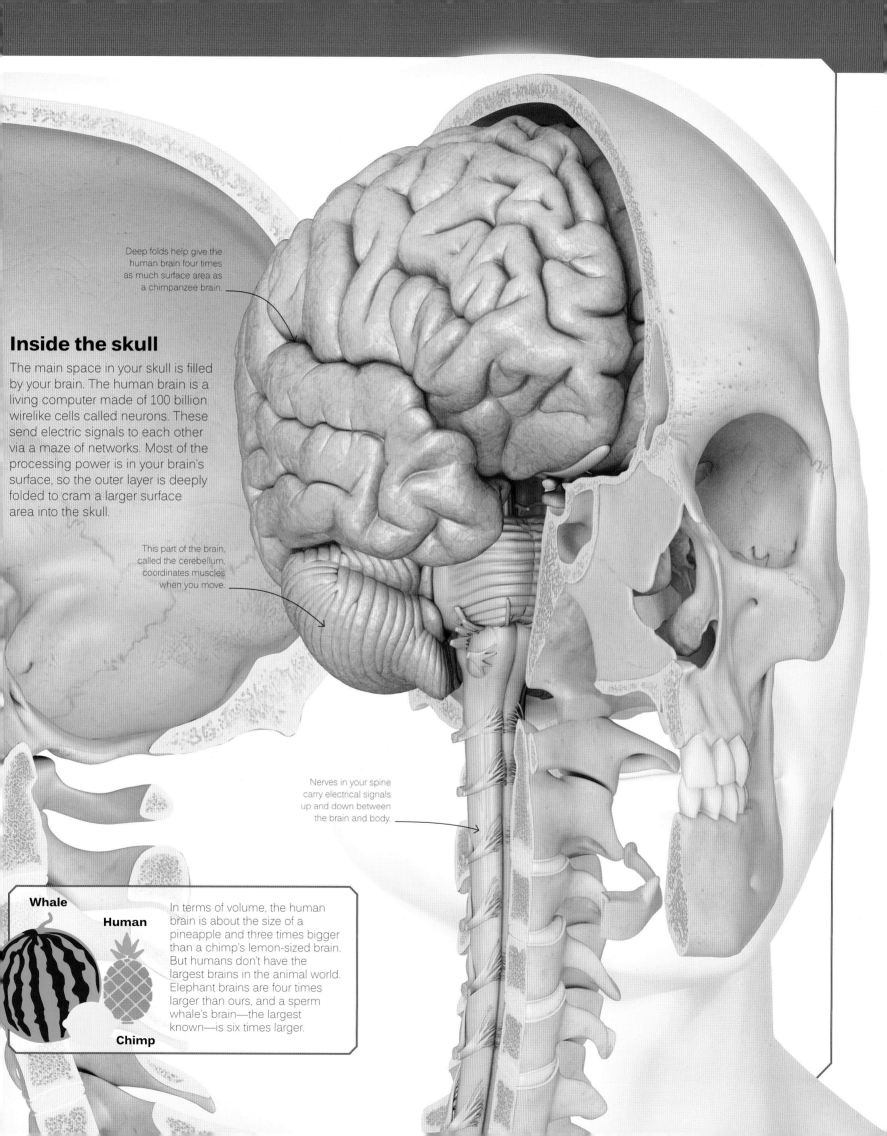

Deep folds help give the human brain four times as much surface area as a chimpanzee brain.

Inside the skull

The main space in your skull is filled by your brain. The human brain is a living computer made of 100 billion wirelike cells called neurons. These send electric signals to each other via a maze of networks. Most of the processing power is in your brain's surface, so the outer layer is deeply folded to cram a larger surface area into the skull.

This part of the brain, called the cerebellum, coordinates muscles when you move.

Nerves in your spine carry electrical signals up and down between the brain and body.

Whale

Human

Chimp

In terms of volume, the human brain is about the size of a pineapple and three times bigger than a chimp's lemon-sized brain. But humans don't have the largest brains in the animal world. Elephant brains are four times larger than ours, and a sperm whale's brain—the largest known—is six times larger.

SUPER SENSES

Some animals, such as sea anemones, survive perfectly well despite having no head, brain, eyes, or ears. However, animals that rely on their wits to survive need sense organs to scan their surroundings for food or danger, and a brain to process that information. In vertebrates, all these organs are clustered near the front of the body, creating a face.

The temporal bone on the side of the skull houses the tiny ear bones.

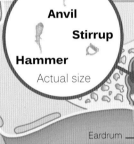

Anvil

Stirrup

Hammer

Actual size

Ear canal

Eardrum →

Cochlea

Ear bones

We owe our sense of hearing to the three smallest bones in the body. Hinged together as levers, these pick up the fluttering vibrations of our eardrums and magnify the force, making our ears much more sensitive to sound. The bones then transmit the vibrations to the fluid-filled cochlea, which converts them into nerve signals for the brain.

Scent detector

Smells are detected deep inside the cavity behind your nose. Here, on the base of your skull, special nerve cells called olfactory receptors capture scent molecules from the air and send signals to your brain. The space in your nose also contains curled shelves of bone called turbinates, which warm and moisten the incoming air, as well as directing some of the air over the olfactory receptors.

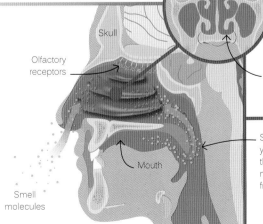

Skull

Olfactory receptors

Cross section through turbinate bones

Mouth

Smells can enter your nose from the back of your mouth as well as from your nostrils.

Smell molecules

Field of view

The position of an animal's eye sockets affects how much it can see at once—its field of view. Eyes on the side of the head give a wide field of view, which helps spot predators. Eyes on the front give a narrow field of view but a wider zone of 3-D vision where the two eyes overlap.

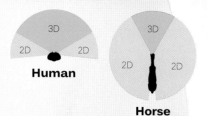

Human

Horse

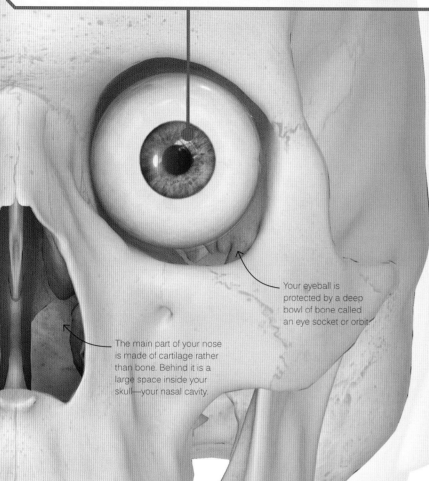

Your eyeball is protected by a deep bowl of bone called an eye socket or orbit

The main part of your nose is made of cartilage rather than bone. Behind it is a large space inside your skull—your nasal cavity.

ANIMAL KINGDOM

Many animals have better senses than ours, or special senses that we don't have at all. Clues to these amazing abilities can often be seen in the animal's skull and face. For example, a long muzzle (nose and mouth) usually means a sharp sense of smell.

Huge eye sockets

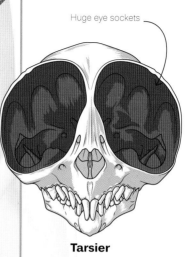

Tarsier

Seeing in the dark

The tarsier is a nighttime hunter in the rainforests of Southeast Asia. Enormous eyes give it superb vision in the dark. The eyes can't move in their sockets, but the tarsier can rotate its head to scan for prey.

The turbinate bones form a series of folds within the nasal cavity.

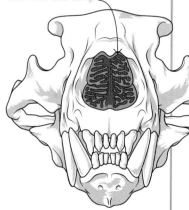

Super smellers

The paper-thin turbinate bones inside a polar bear's nose form a mazelike structure through which scents pass. Polar bears have 20 times more smell cells than we have and can sniff out prey such as seals from 6 miles (10 km) away.

Polar bear

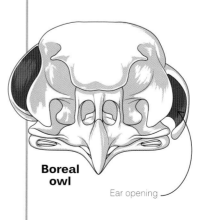

Boreal owl

Ear opening

3-D hearing

Some owls have one ear higher than the other. This unusual feature helps an owl work out the precise location of mice hidden deep under leaves or snow by listening to them move. The owl's dish-shaped face also helps collect and channel faint sounds to its ears.

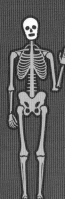
OPEN WIDE

Compared to the teeth of other animals, ours seem surprisingly small and unimpressive. We lack the fearsome, stabbing canines of a carnivore or the heavy-duty grinding teeth of an herbivore. Our teeth resemble those of our ape relatives, but even they have bigger teeth than we do. This might be because early humans mastered stone tools to pound and cut up food, and fire to cook and soften it. Our ancestors no longer needed big, powerful teeth, so over time they became smaller.

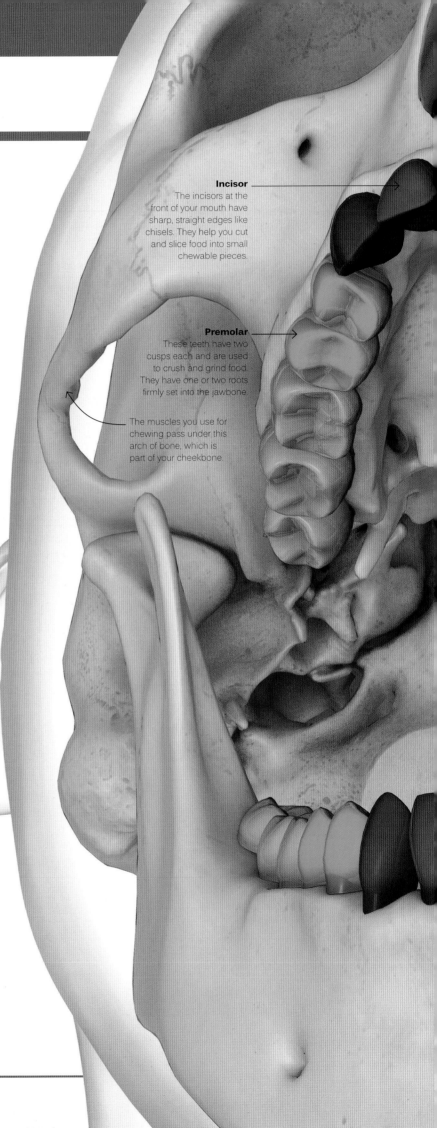

Incisor
The incisors at the front of your mouth have sharp, straight edges like chisels. They help you cut and slice food into small chewable pieces.

Premolar
These teeth have two cusps each and are used to crush and grind food. They have one or two roots firmly set into the jawbone.

The muscles you use for chewing pass under this arch of bone, which is part of your cheekbone.

Biting and chewing

Anchored to either side of the skull are two powerful muscles—the temporalis and the masseter. These work together when you bite and chew food. They also move the lower jaw sideways to help grind food—something carnivorous animals cannot do.

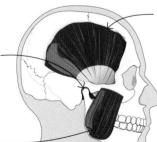

A disk of cartilage in this hinge joint cushions the jawbone when you chew.

The fan-shaped temporalis muscle helps crush food between your molars.

The masseter is one of the strongest muscles of the body. It helps close the jaw.

DO TRY THIS AT HOME

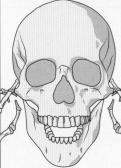

Your jaw joints are more than simple hinges. As the lower jaw opens, it also slides forward slightly from its socket in the skull. This helps the jaw move in three ways—up and down, side to side, and forward and backward. You can feel your jaw pop out of its socket by pressing your fingertips in front of your ears and opening your mouth—your fingers will sink into soft pits where the bone was.

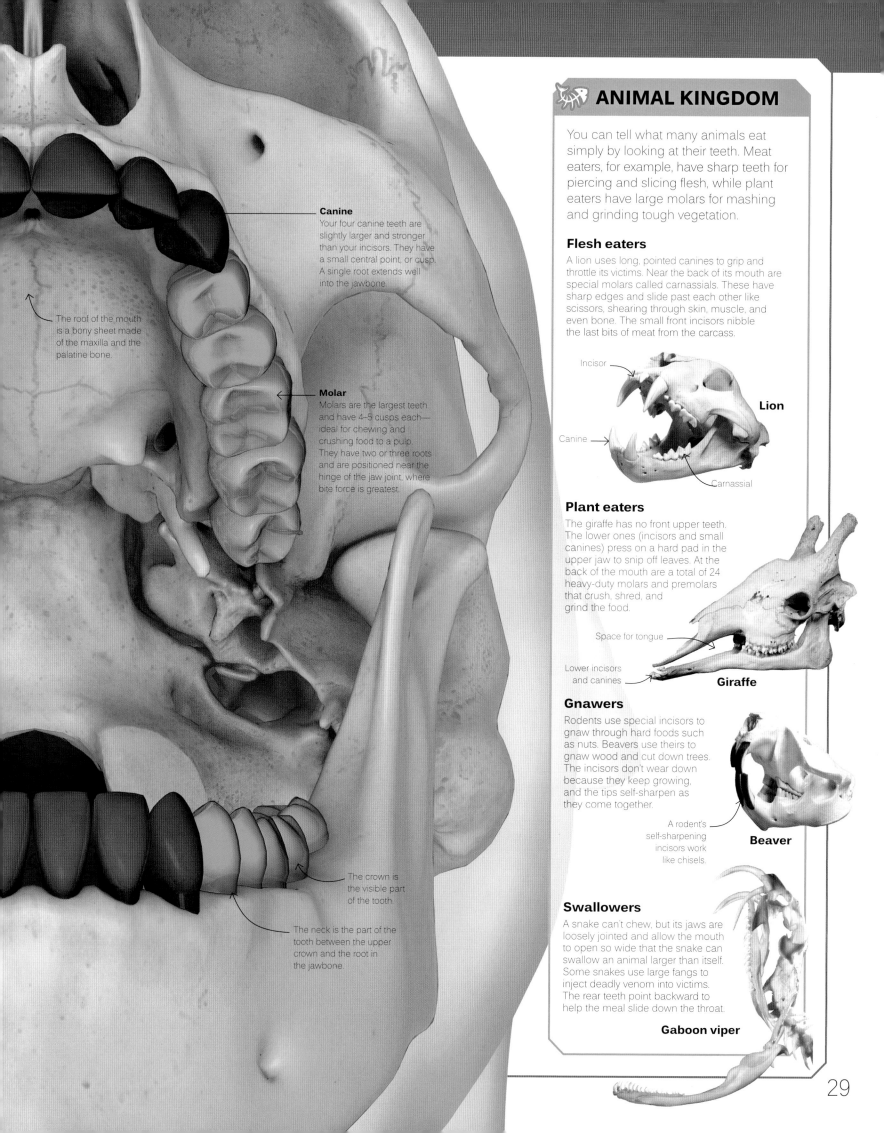

Canine
Your four canine teeth are slightly larger and stronger than your incisors. They have a small central point, or cusp. A single root extends well into the jawbone.

The roof of the mouth is a bony sheet made of the maxilla and the palatine bone.

Molar
Molars are the largest teeth and have 4–5 cusps each—ideal for chewing and crushing food to a pulp. They have two or three roots and are positioned near the hinge of the jaw joint, where bite force is greatest.

The crown is the visible part of the tooth.

The neck is the part of the tooth between the upper crown and the root in the jawbone.

ANIMAL KINGDOM

You can tell what many animals eat simply by looking at their teeth. Meat eaters, for example, have sharp teeth for piercing and slicing flesh, while plant eaters have large molars for mashing and grinding tough vegetation.

Flesh eaters

A lion uses long, pointed canines to grip and throttle its victims. Near the back of its mouth are special molars called carnassials. These have sharp edges and slide past each other like scissors, shearing through skin, muscle, and even bone. The small front incisors nibble the last bits of meat from the carcass.

Incisor

Canine

Lion

Carnassial

Plant eaters

The giraffe has no front upper teeth. The lower ones (incisors and small canines) press on a hard pad in the upper jaw to snip off leaves. At the back of the mouth are a total of 24 heavy-duty molars and premolars that crush, shred, and grind the food.

Space for tongue

Lower incisors and canines

Giraffe

Gnawers

Rodents use special incisors to gnaw through hard foods such as nuts. Beavers use theirs to gnaw wood and cut down trees. The incisors don't wear down because they keep growing, and the tips self-sharpen as they come together.

A rodent's self-sharpening incisors work like chisels.

Beaver

Swallowers

A snake can't chew, but its jaws are loosely jointed and allow the mouth to open so wide that the snake can swallow an animal larger than itself. Some snakes use large fangs to inject deadly venom into victims. The rear teeth point backward to help the meal slide down the throat.

Gaboon viper

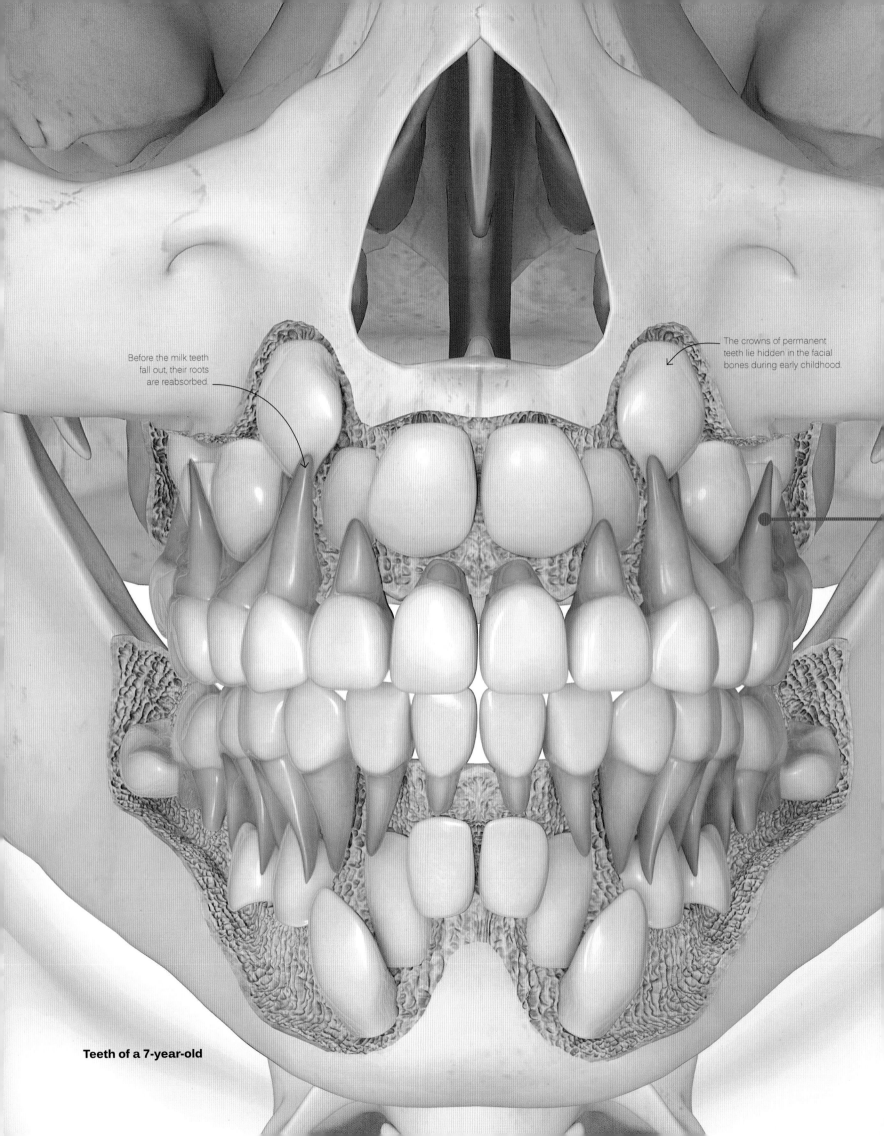

Before the milk teeth fall out, their roots are reabsorbed.

The crowns of permanent teeth lie hidden in the facial bones during early childhood.

Teeth of a 7-year-old

Inside a tooth

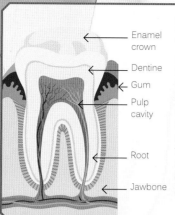

Enamel crown
Dentine
Gum
Pulp cavity
Root
Jawbone

Teeth get their strength from crystals of calcium phosphate, the mineral that makes bones hard. The crown of a tooth is 96 percent calcium phosphate and forms a brittle material called enamel—the hardest substance in the body. Beneath this is a bonelike tissue called dentine, and inside that is a cavity containing blood vessels and pain-sensitive nerve cells.

ANIMAL KINGDOM

With a few exceptions, most mammals have two sets of teeth in their life, but many reptiles and fish continuously grow new teeth as their old ones fall out.

Six sets

An elephant grows six sets of molars during its life. New molars appear at the back of the jaw and slowly move to the front, pushing older teeth out. After the last set of molars falls out, the elephant will die of starvation.

An elephant's tusks are special teeth.

Elephant

Fifty sets

A crocodile's 60 or so teeth are replaced about 50 times in its life, so a crocodile may get through 3,000 teeth. Crocodile teeth aren't worn down by chewing, since crocodiles swallow mouthfuls of flesh whole, but their teeth can be ripped out by prey struggling to escape.

Crocodile

Endless teeth

The skin inside a shark's mouth grows toward its lips like a conveyor belt, constantly carrying razor-sharp new teeth to replace the old ones. A shark may get through 30,000 teeth in a lifetime.

Shark

Disposable teeth

Your first set of 20 teeth are called milk teeth or baby teeth. As you get older, the roots of milk teeth are reabsorbed and the crowns fall out, allowing permanent teeth to replace them. By the age of 11, most children have no milk teeth left. Although milk teeth are temporary, it's important to take care of them because they help guide the growing permanent teeth into place. The last permanent teeth—wisdom teeth—appear in your late teens.

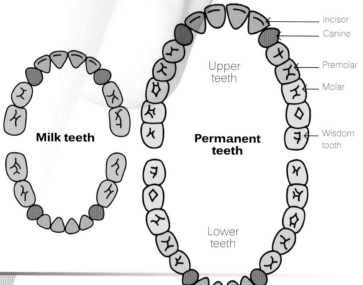

Incisor
Canine
Premolar
Molar
Wisdom tooth

Milk teeth

Permanent teeth

Upper teeth

Lower teeth

GROWING TEETH

By the time we reach about seven years old, all the teeth we will ever have are already in our skulls, though most are hidden from view. We grow two sets of teeth: milk teeth (baby teeth) and permanent teeth. Both begin forming long before birth, developing from buds embedded deep in the bone of the skull. The first set starts to force its way through the gums when a baby is about six months old. The second set begins to emerge around six years later.

Skull-piercing tusks

The babirusa is a piglike animal from the rainforests of Indonesia. The male's top canines grow upward, touch its face, and then curve back. In old males, the tusks may even pierce the animal's skull and kill it.

Babirusa

Unicorn of the sea

The narwhal is a whale that lives in Arctic waters. One of its canine teeth grows into a long spiral tusk, the purpose of which is a mystery. The tusk has no enamel but lots of nerves, so it might be a sense organ. Another theory is that rival males use their tusks in jousting battles.

Narwhal

FLEXIBLE NECK

From gerbils to giraffes, nearly all mammals have the same number of bones in their necks: seven. These seven sturdy bones, called neck vertebrae, make up the top part of the spine. Your neck bones allow your head to move, but they also protect your spinal cord—the vital cable of nerves that links your brain to your body, allowing you to control your muscles.

Giraffes have the same number of neck bones as **humans.**

Your skull is tied to your neck bones by a thick band of fibrous tissue called the nuchal ligament. This stops your head from tipping forward when you run. In fast-running animals, this ligament is very large and is called a paddywhack.

Atlas

Peg

Axis

Tilt and turn

The first two vertebrae are specially shaped to let your head swivel. The first one (the atlas) fits over a kind of peg in the second one (the axis) like a washer over a bolt. This allows your head to swivel around—handy for saying no. Another joint between the base of the skull and the atlas lets you nod your head yes.

Atlas

Axis

☝ DO TRY THIS AT HOME

Your neck bones have enough flexibility to turn your head through about a half circle without moving your shoulders. By moving your eyes, you can see in a complete circle. To try this yourself, place a small object directly behind you and then try looking at it from both sides (but don't twist your waist or shoulders).

Spurs of bone on each vertebra provide attachment sites for the nuchal ligament and for the muscles that move the head.

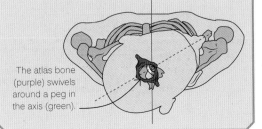

The atlas bone (purple) swivels around a peg in the axis (green).

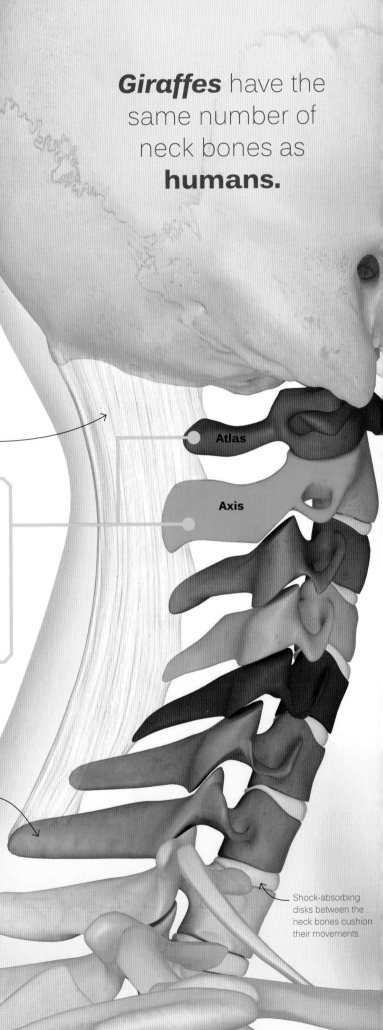

Shock-absorbing disks between the neck bones cushion their movements.

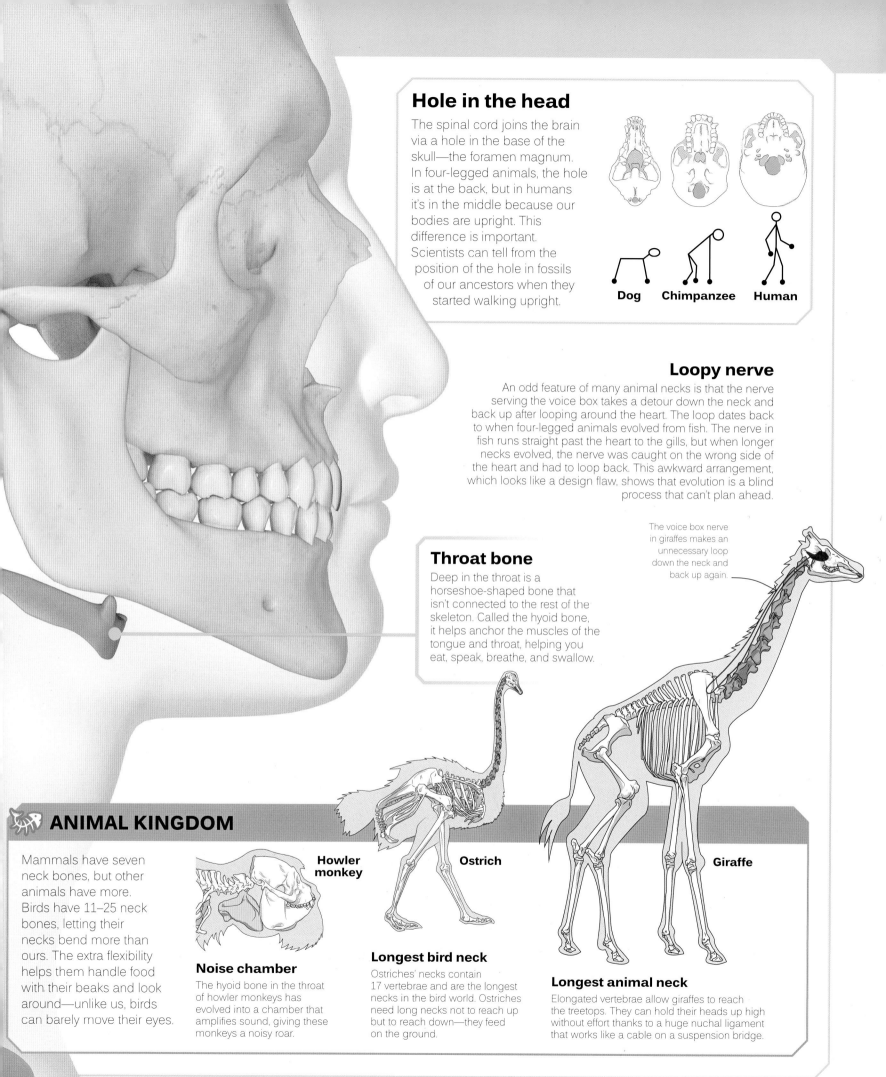

Hole in the head

The spinal cord joins the brain via a hole in the base of the skull—the foramen magnum. In four-legged animals, the hole is at the back, but in humans it's in the middle because our bodies are upright. This difference is important. Scientists can tell from the position of the hole in fossils of our ancestors when they started walking upright.

Dog   **Chimpanzee**   **Human**

Loopy nerve

An odd feature of many animal necks is that the nerve serving the voice box takes a detour down the neck and back up after looping around the heart. The loop dates back to when four-legged animals evolved from fish. The nerve in fish runs straight past the heart to the gills, but when longer necks evolved, the nerve was caught on the wrong side of the heart and had to loop back. This awkward arrangement, which looks like a design flaw, shows that evolution is a blind process that can't plan ahead.

The voice box nerve in giraffes makes an unnecessary loop down the neck and back up again.

Throat bone

Deep in the throat is a horseshoe-shaped bone that isn't connected to the rest of the skeleton. Called the hyoid bone, it helps anchor the muscles of the tongue and throat, helping you eat, speak, breathe, and swallow.

Ostrich

Giraffe

ANIMAL KINGDOM

Mammals have seven neck bones, but other animals have more. Birds have 11–25 neck bones, letting their necks bend more than ours. The extra flexibility helps them handle food with their beaks and look around—unlike us, birds can barely move their eyes.

Howler monkey

Noise chamber

The hyoid bone in the throat of howler monkeys has evolved into a chamber that amplifies sound, giving these monkeys a noisy roar.

Longest bird neck

Ostriches' necks contain 17 vertebrae and are the longest necks in the bird world. Ostriches need long necks not to reach up but to reach down—they feed on the ground.

Longest animal neck

Elongated vertebrae allow giraffes to reach the treetops. They can hold their heads up high without effort thanks to a huge nuchal ligament that works like a cable on a suspension bridge.

SPINAL COLUMN

Run your fingers down the middle of your back. The knobby bumps you can feel are your vertebrae—33 interlocking bones that make up your spinal column, or backbone. This is the main supporting structure in the skeleton and carries the weight of your upper body. It also houses and protects the spinal cord—a vital cable of nerves running between your brain and the rest of your body.

Double bend

In most mammals, the backbone is a horizontal arch that supports the body like a bridge, but ours is different because we walk on two legs. To keep us balanced, our backbone has an extra bend near the bottom that curves forward. This develops at the age of one when we start to walk.

Neck bones

The top seven bones in the spine (called cervical vertebrae) form the neck.

Chest bones

The next 12 bones (thoracic vertebrae) form the back of the chest. Each one is joined to a pair of ribs.

Lower back

Five large, sturdy bones (called lumbar vertebrae) make up the lower back. In humans these create a forward bend.

Hip connection

The spine is joined to the hip bones by a triangular bone called the sacrum. This is made of 5 vertebrae that fuse together around the age of 18.

Tailbone

Between three and five small vertebrae make up the tailbone (coccyx).

Joints between the spine and ribs allow your chest to rise and fall when you breathe deeply.

Muscles and ligaments attach to the wing-shaped "processes" on the back of each vertebra.

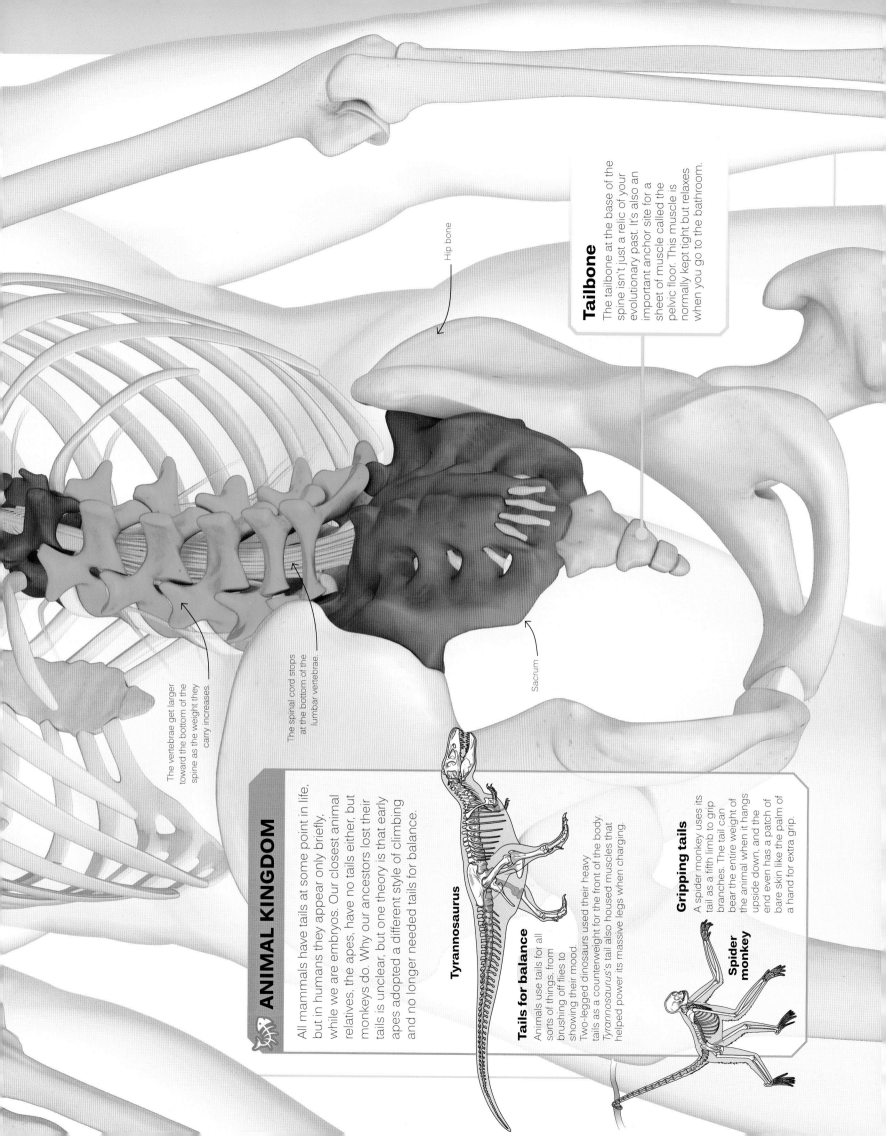

Hip bone

Sacrum

The vertebrae get larger toward the bottom of the spine as the weight they carry increases.

The spinal cord stops at the bottom of the lumbar vertebrae.

Tailbone

The tailbone at the base of the spine isn't just a relic of your evolutionary past. It's also an important anchor site for a sheet of muscle called the pelvic floor. This muscle is normally kept tight but relaxes when you go to the bathroom.

ANIMAL KINGDOM

All mammals have tails at some point in life, but in humans they appear only briefly, while we are embryos. Our closest animal relatives, the apes, have no tails either, but monkeys do. Why our ancestors lost their tails is unclear, but one theory is that early apes adopted a different style of climbing and no longer needed tails for balance.

Tyrannosaurus

Tails for balance

Animals use tails for all sorts of things, from brushing off flies to showing their mood. Two-legged dinosaurs used their heavy tails as a counterweight for the front of the body. *Tyrannosaurus's* tail also housed muscles that helped power its massive legs when charging.

Gripping tails

A spider monkey uses its tail as a fifth limb to grip branches. The tail can bear the entire weight of the animal when it hangs upside down, and the end even has a patch of bare skin like the palm of a hand for extra grip.

Spider monkey

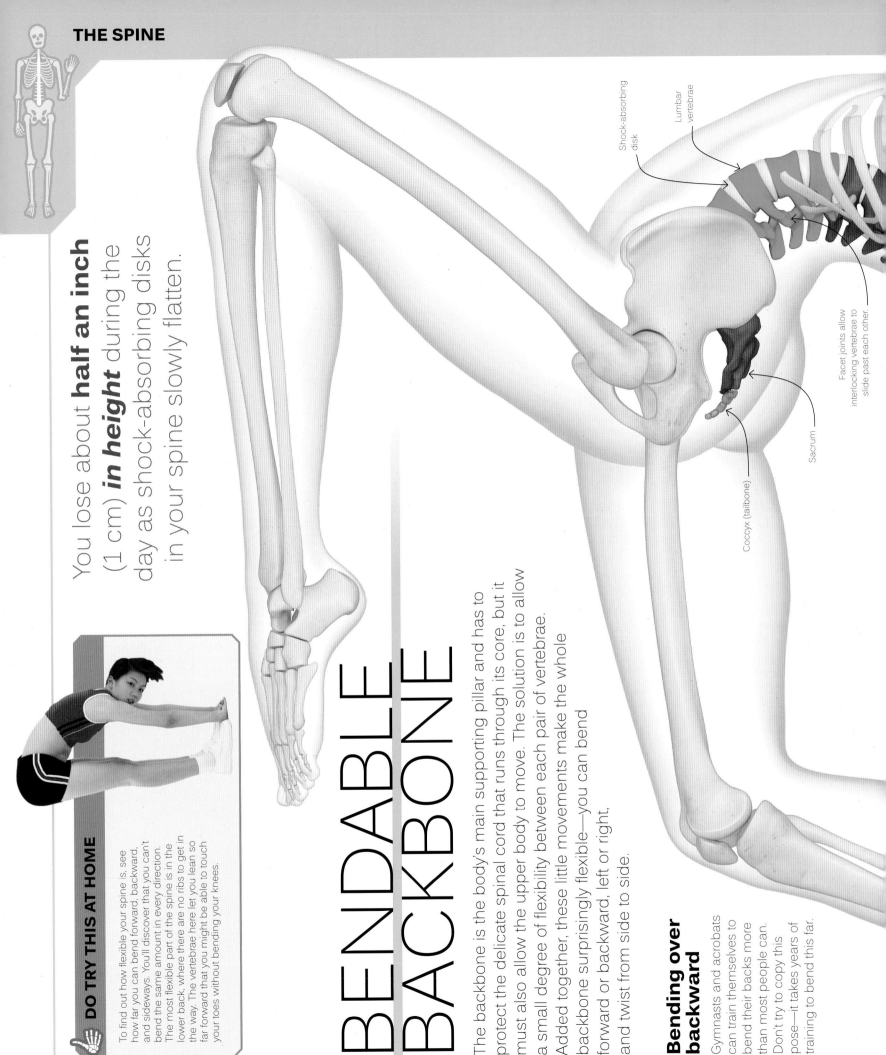

Shock-absorbing disk

Lumbar vertebrae

Facet joints allow interlocking vertebrae to slide past each other.

Sacrum

Coccyx (tailbone)

You lose about **half an inch** *(1 cm) in height* during the day as shock-absorbing disks in your spine slowly flatten.

DO TRY THIS AT HOME

To find out how flexible your spine is, see how far you can bend forward, backward, and sideways. You'll discover that you can't bend the same amount in every direction. The most flexible part of the spine is in the lower back, where there are no ribs to get in the way. The vertebrae here let you lean so far forward that you might be able to touch your toes without bending your knees.

BENDABLE BACKBONE

The backbone is the body's main supporting pillar and has to protect the delicate spinal cord that runs through its core, but it must also allow the upper body to move. The solution is to allow a small degree of flexibility between each pair of vertebrae. Added together, these little movements make the whole backbone surprisingly flexible—you can bend forward or backward, left or right, and twist from side to side.

Bending over backward

Gymnasts and acrobats can train themselves to bend their backs more than most people can. Don't try to copy this pose—it takes years of training to bend this far.

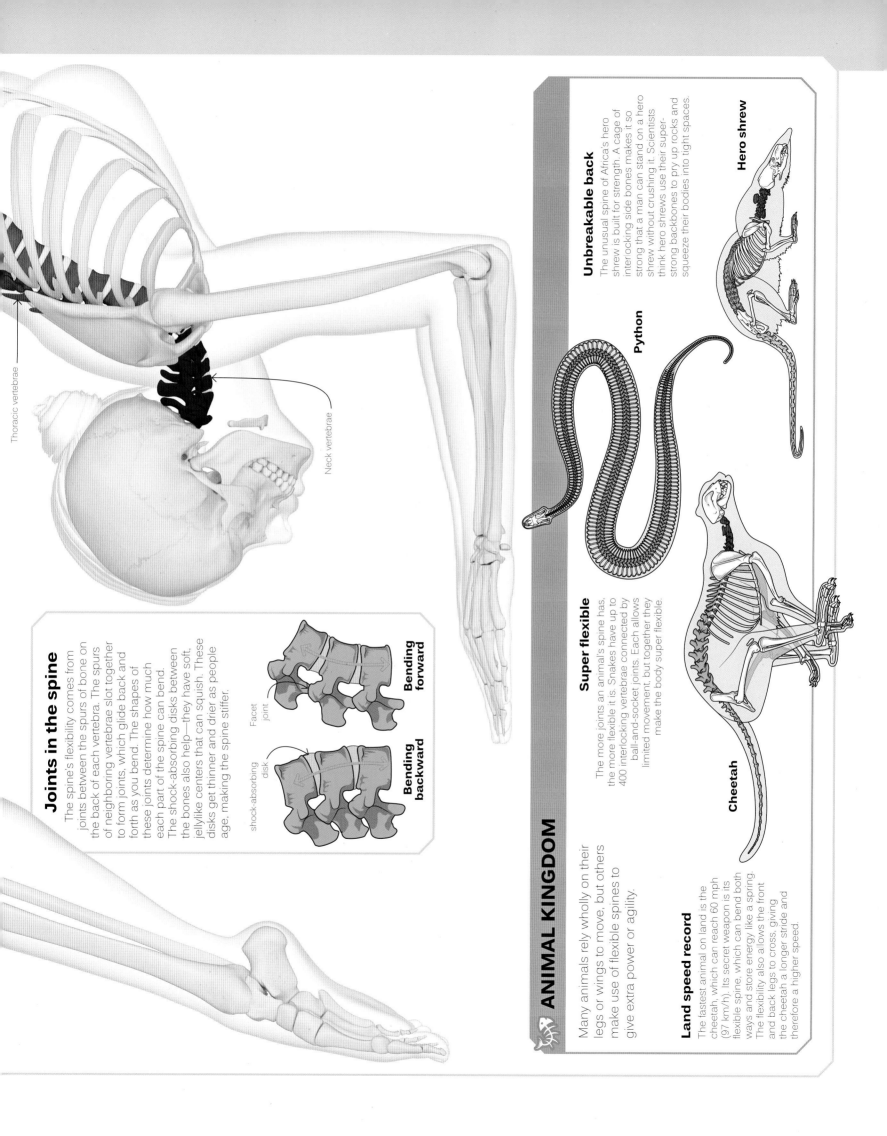

Thoracic vertebrae

Neck vertebrae

Joints in the spine

The spine's flexibility comes from joints between the spurs of bone on the back of each vertebra. The spurs of neighboring vertebrae slot together to form joints, which glide back and forth as you bend. The shapes of these joints determine how much each part of the spine can bend. The shock-absorbing disks between the bones also help—they have soft, jellylike centers that can squish. These disks get thinner and drier as people age, making the spine stiffer.

shock-absorbing disk

Facet joint

Bending backward

Bending forward

ANIMAL KINGDOM

Many animals rely wholly on their legs or wings to move, but others make use of flexible spines to give extra power or agility.

Land speed record

The fastest animal on land is the cheetah, which can reach 60 mph (97 km/h). Its secret weapon is its flexible spine, which can bend both ways and store energy like a spring. The flexibility also allows the front and back legs to cross, giving the cheetah a longer stride and therefore a higher speed.

Cheetah

Super flexible

The more joints an animal's spine has, the more flexible it is. Snakes have up to 400 interlocking vertebrae connected by ball-and-socket joints. Each allows limited movement, but together they make the body super flexible.

Python

Unbreakable back

The unusual spine of Africa's hero shrew is built for strength. A cage of interlocking side bones makes it so strong that a man can stand on a hero shrew without crushing it. Scientists think hero shrews use their super-strong backbones to pry up rocks and squeeze their bodies into tight spaces.

Hero shrew

SHOULDER SUPPORT

Sometimes a part of an animal's body that evolved to do a particular job turns out, with a little tweaking, to be ideal for something entirely different. This happened with the human shoulder—the most mobile joint in the body. We inherited our super-flexible shoulders from apes that used theirs for climbing in trees. When our ancestors left the trees, flexible shoulders turned out to be useful for all sorts of other tasks, from carrying babies to wielding weapons.

Shoulder bones

Three major bones meet in your shoulder: the humerus in your upper arm; the shoulder blade on your back; and the collarbone on your front. All three provide anchorage for the powerful muscles that move the arm.

Built to throw

Unlike most meat-eating mammals, humans have no built-in hunting weapons such as claws or large canine teeth. Instead, our prehistoric ancestors relied on rocks and spears to kill their prey. The ability to swing arms overhead made humans better at throwing than any other animal. Even apes are no match. A chimpanzee can fling a ball at about 20 mph (32 km/h), but a 12-year-old child can triple that speed, and a professional baseball pitcher can throw at 105 mph (169 km/h).

First shoulders

Shoulders made their first appearance in the history of life around 400 million years ago, when shallow-water fish began to develop legs that helped them wriggle over mud. Their delicate fin bones became sturdier and fewer in number, forming fingers and toes, and their skulls separated to create a shoulder girdle, anchoring the forelimbs and allowing them to move separately from the head. This major change paved the way for the colonization of land.

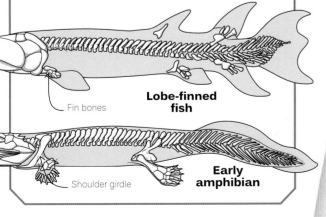

Fin bones

Lobe-finned fish

Shoulder girdle

Early amphibian

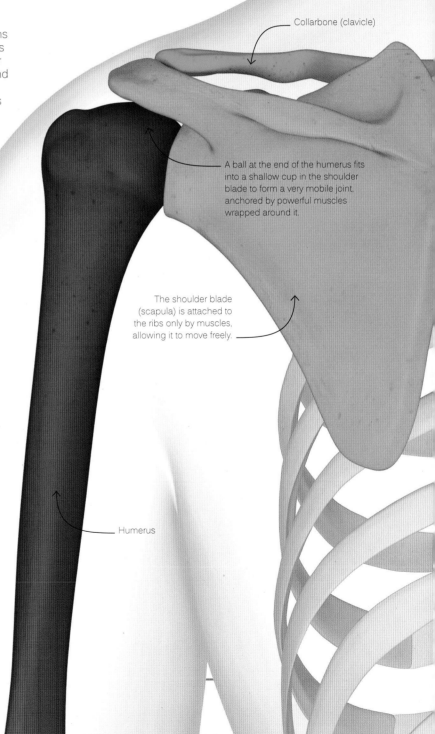

Collarbone (clavicle)

A ball at the end of the humerus fits into a shallow cup in the shoulder blade to form a very mobile joint, anchored by powerful muscles wrapped around it.

The shoulder blade (scapula) is attached to the ribs only by muscles, allowing it to move freely.

Humerus

Because shoulders provide anchorage for an animal's forelimbs, their structure reflects the way each species moves. As our tree-dwelling ancestors became more upright, their shoulders became more mobile.

Built for speed

Most four-legged mammals are built to run quickly. The shoulders of dogs and wolves work more like hinges than ours do, allowing the legs to swing powerfully forward and backward but preventing them from reaching overhead. The shoulder blade is long and narrow, giving a long stride, and the collarbone is absent, allowing the shoulder blade to swing.

The shoulder blade is on the side of the body.

Gray wolf

Monkey business

Most monkeys scamper around on all fours with a doglike posture. Their shoulder blades are on the sides of the body, as in dogs, but monkeys have a more triangular scapula and a collarbone to provide anchorage for climbing muscles.

Triangular shoulder blade

Rhesus monkey

White-handed gibbon

King of the swingers

In apes (the group of animals that humans belong to), the triangular shoulder blades have moved to the back, freeing up the arms to reach overhead. Apes tend to move around with an upright chest, unlike monkeys. Some apes move by swinging gracefully beneath branches. Others use muscular arms to reach overhead and haul themselves up tree trunks.

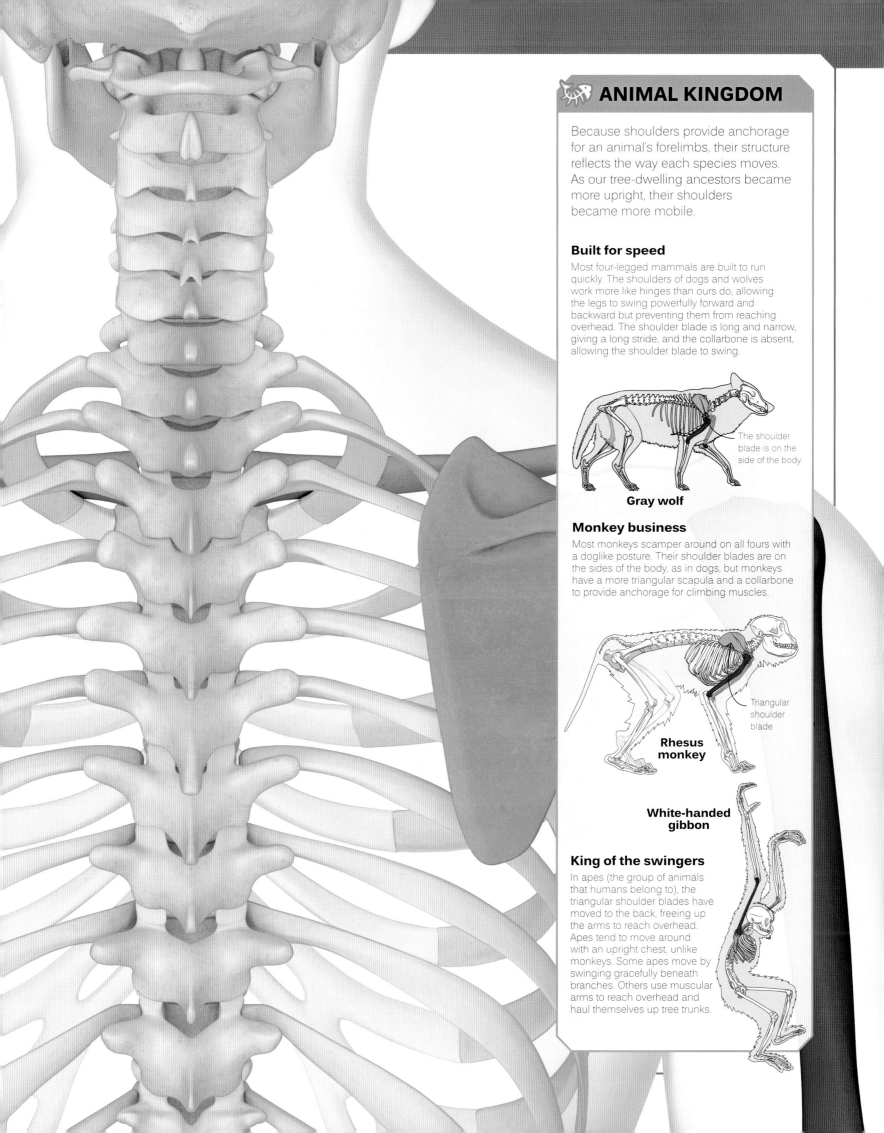

ANIMAL KINGDOM

The limbs of all vertebrates other than fish are based on the same structure, with three main bones and five digits (fingers or toes). Evolution has adapted this structure in many different ways.

Flippers

Whales and dolphins use their flattened forelimbs as flippers for steering. They look different from our arms, but contain nearly all the same bones. In contrast, the bones of their unused hind limbs have shrunk over millions of years to tiny relics.

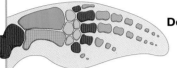

Dolphin

Diggers

Moles have fantastically powerful forelimbs and large six-fingered hands to use as shovels for digging. The "sixth finger," which is not a true finger, evolved from a minor thumb bone that is tiny in human hands. The humerus is hook-shaped to provide anchorage for the powerful digging muscles.

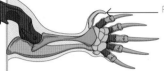

False finger

Mole

Wings

Birds evolved from small predatory dinosaurs whose grasping hands had only three fingers each. All three fingers are still present, but two are much smaller than the other.

Eagle

ADAPTABLE ARMS

One striking difference between humans and other animals is that we have a spare pair of large, powerful limbs dangling from the body: our arms. In most animals, the front limbs are specialized to move the body around, whether by walking, flying, swimming, or climbing. Ours, however, are free to serve as multipurpose devices that can adapt to do many jobs. Just three long bones form the main part of the arm. They work together with the 27 bones of the hand and wrist to make the human arm incredibly adaptable.

Humerus

The longest bone in the arm is the humerus. At its upper end is the extremely mobile shoulder joint, while its lower end forms part of the elbow, which is a simple hinge joint.

People call the elbow end of the humerus the "funny bone" because bumping it squeezes a nerve, causing a sensation like an electric shock.

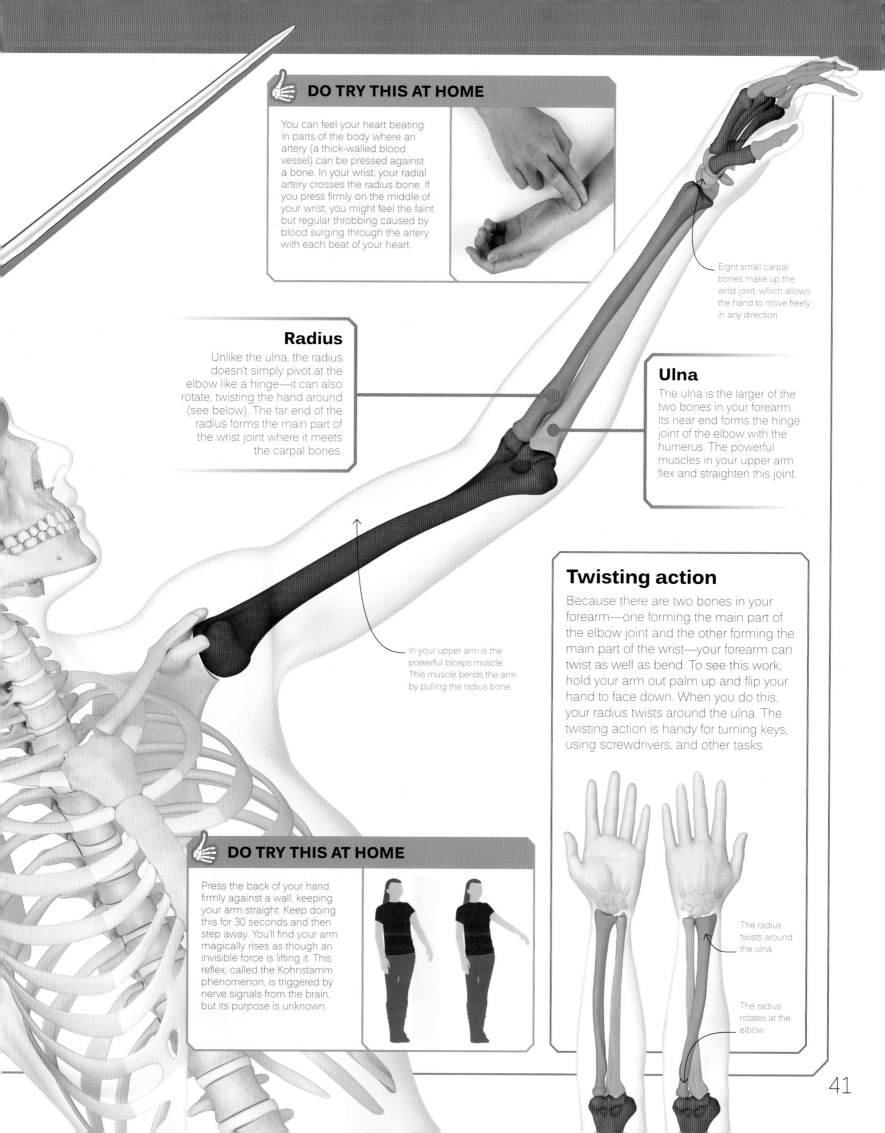

DO TRY THIS AT HOME

You can feel your heart beating in parts of the body where an artery (a thick-walled blood vessel) can be pressed against a bone. In your wrist, your radial artery crosses the radius bone. If you press firmly on the middle of your wrist, you might feel the faint but regular throbbing caused by blood surging through the artery with each beat of your heart.

Eight small carpal bones make up the wrist joint, which allows the hand to move freely in any direction.

Radius

Unlike the ulna, the radius doesn't simply pivot at the elbow like a hinge—it can also rotate, twisting the hand around (see below). The far end of the radius forms the main part of the wrist joint where it meets the carpal bones.

Ulna

The ulna is the larger of the two bones in your forearm. Its near end forms the hinge joint of the elbow with the humerus. The powerful muscles in your upper arm flex and straighten this joint.

In your upper arm is the powerful biceps muscle. This muscle bends the arm by pulling the radius bone.

Twisting action

Because there are two bones in your forearm—one forming the main part of the elbow joint and the other forming the main part of the wrist—your forearm can twist as well as bend. To see this work, hold your arm out palm up and flip your hand to face down. When you do this, your radius twists around the ulna. The twisting action is handy for turning keys, using screwdrivers, and other tasks.

DO TRY THIS AT HOME

Press the back of your hand firmly against a wall, keeping your arm straight. Keep doing this for 30 seconds and then step away. You'll find your arm magically rises as though an invisible force is lifting it. This reflex, called the Kohnstamm phenomenon, is triggered by nerve signals from the brain, but its purpose is unknown.

The radius twists around the ulna.

The radius rotates at the elbow.

Motor skills

Human hands can do many different things, but the skills don't come automatically—you have to practice. It can take weeks to be able to click your fingers or tie shoelaces, and years to learn to play a musical instrument. Practicing causes the parts of your brain that control muscles to rewire themselves, creating what scientists call motor skills. Once you've mastered a motor skill, it stays with you for life.

Five bones called metacarpals make up the palm of your hand and the base of your thumb.

Simple hinge joints connect your finger bones.

Your wrist is made up of eight bones called carpals.

Your fingers and thumbs are made up of bones called phalanges—three in each finger but only two in each thumb.

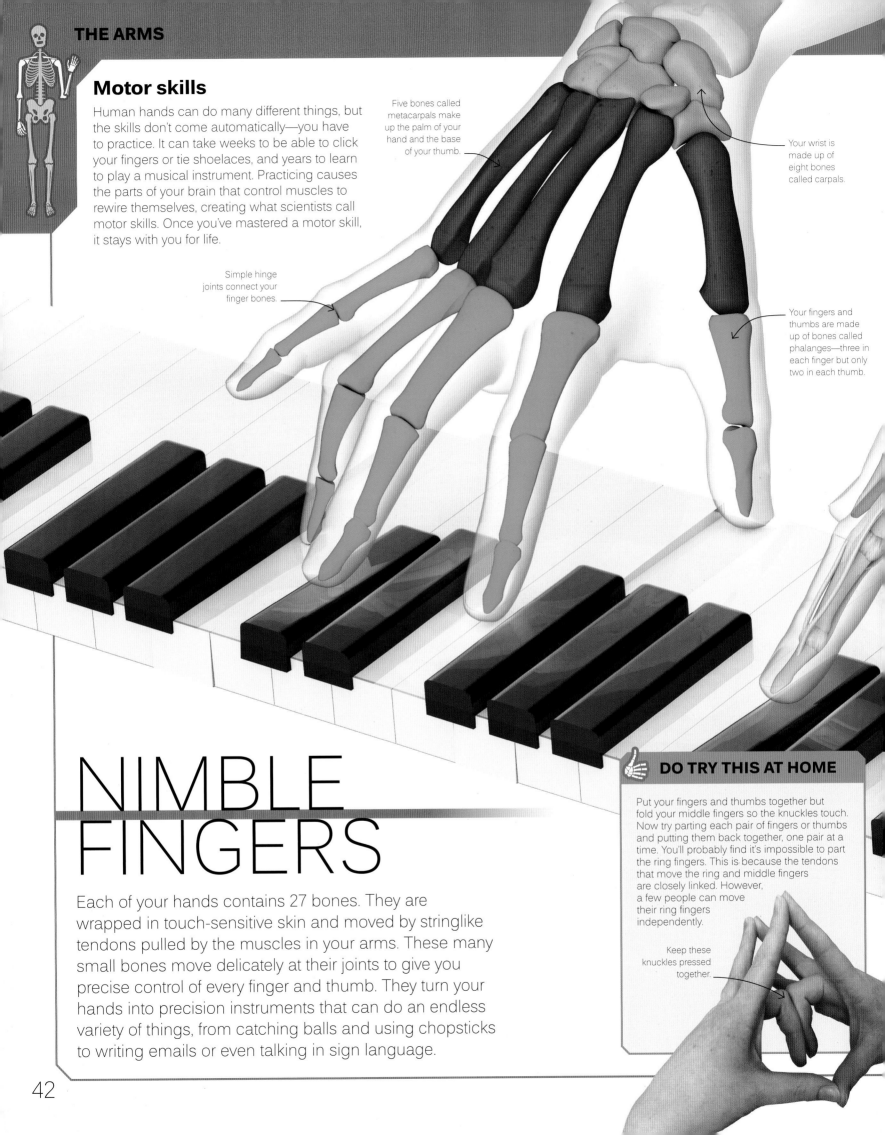

NIMBLE FINGERS

Each of your hands contains 27 bones. They are wrapped in touch-sensitive skin and moved by stringlike tendons pulled by the muscles in your arms. These many small bones move delicately at their joints to give you precise control of every finger and thumb. They turn your hands into precision instruments that can do an endless variety of things, from catching balls and using chopsticks to writing emails or even talking in sign language.

DO TRY THIS AT HOME

Put your fingers and thumbs together but fold your middle fingers so the knuckles touch. Now try parting each pair of fingers or thumbs and putting them back together, one pair at a time. You'll probably find it's impossible to part the ring fingers. This is because the tendons that move the ring and middle fingers are closely linked. However, a few people can move their ring fingers independently.

Keep these knuckles pressed together.

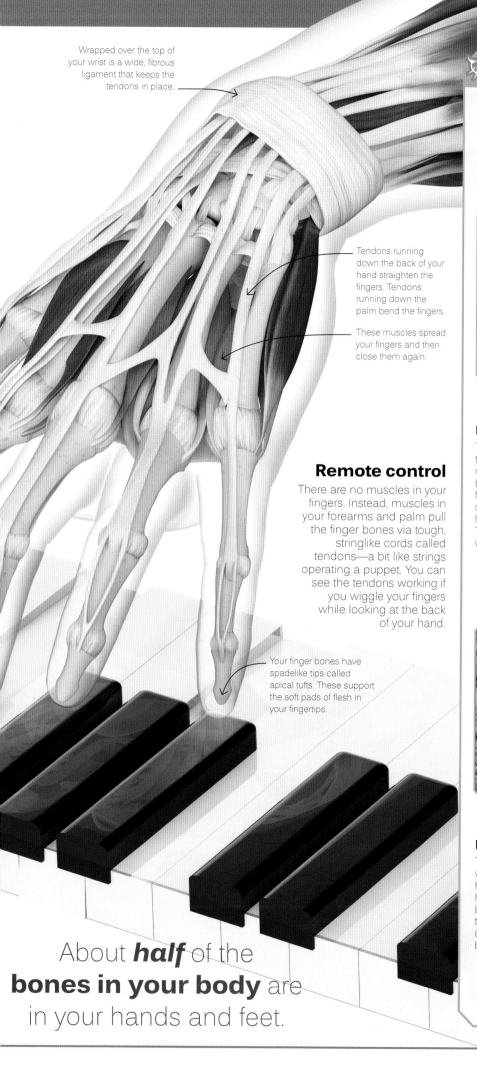

Wrapped over the top of your wrist is a wide, fibrous ligament that keeps the tendons in place.

Tendons running down the back of your hand straighten the fingers. Tendons running down the palm bend the fingers.

These muscles spread your fingers and then close them again.

Remote control

There are no muscles in your fingers. Instead, muscles in your forearms and palm pull the finger bones via tough, stringlike cords called tendons—a bit like strings operating a puppet. You can see the tendons working if you wiggle your fingers while looking at the back of your hand.

Your finger bones have spadelike tips called apical tufts. These support the soft pads of flesh in your fingertips.

About **half** of the **bones in your body** are in your hands and feet.

ANIMAL KINGDOM

Most four-legged animals use their front feet as platforms for walking on. Humans are different because walking upright left our hands free for other things. However, we are not the only animals to have found new uses for our front feet.

Grub hook

The aye-aye's twig-shaped middle finger is much thinner than the others. It pokes this finger deep into rotten wood to pull out beetle grubs with its claw. To locate them first, it taps the wood and listens with large, batlike ears.

Aye-aye

Flying fingers

The finger bones of bats form the framework of their delicate, membranous wings. As well as being extraordinarily long, bats' finger bones are softer than those of other mammals because they have lower levels of calcium. This helps them flex with each wingbeat, powering their flight.

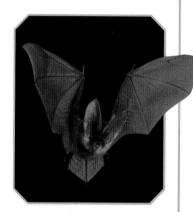

Gray long-eared bat

Handy hooks

Sloths' fingers have long, curved claws that they use as hooks to hang from trees. They can even sleep like this. All sloths have three toes on their hind feet, but the so-called two-toed sloths have only two fingers on each hand, while three-toed sloths have three.

Three-toed sloth

Fly catchers

Tarsiers have long fingers tipped with wide pads that are not only handy for gripping trees but also help them catch prey. They hunt by leaping after prey and using their outstretched fingers as cages to snatch flying insects, bats, and even birds in midair.

Philippine tarsier

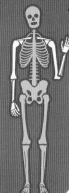
PRECISION GRIP

Pinch your thumb together with the tip of each finger. It's a simple action, but it's something that other mammals—even those with five fingers like us—cannot do. It gives us the ability to pick up and handle objects with a precision and dexterity that no animal can match. Without this unique skill, humans could never have invented the tools and technologies that allowed us to become so successful.

The thick pad of soft flesh on the tip of your thumb can mold around objects for better grip.

Opposable thumbs

Because thumbs move the opposite way from fingers, we call them opposable. We inherited this feature from tree-dwelling primates that use opposable thumbs to climb. After our ancestors left the trees, grasping hands proved useful for holding tools, and our hands changed to become better at manipulating objects: the thumb got longer and the fingers shorter, allowing the tips to meet.

50 percent of the brain area that controls your hands is devoted to your **thumbs**.

At the base of the thumb is a saddle joint, so called because the bones fit together like a rider on a horse. This joint lets the thumb swing in any direction but stops it from twisting.

DO TRY THIS AT HOME

To see how useful thumbs are, ask a friend to tape yours to the sides of your hands so you can't use them. Then try doing some of the following things with just your fingers:

- Turn on a faucet
- Bounce a ball
- Peel a banana
- Eat an apple
- Button a shirt
- Write your name
- Blow up a balloon
- Tie your shoelaces

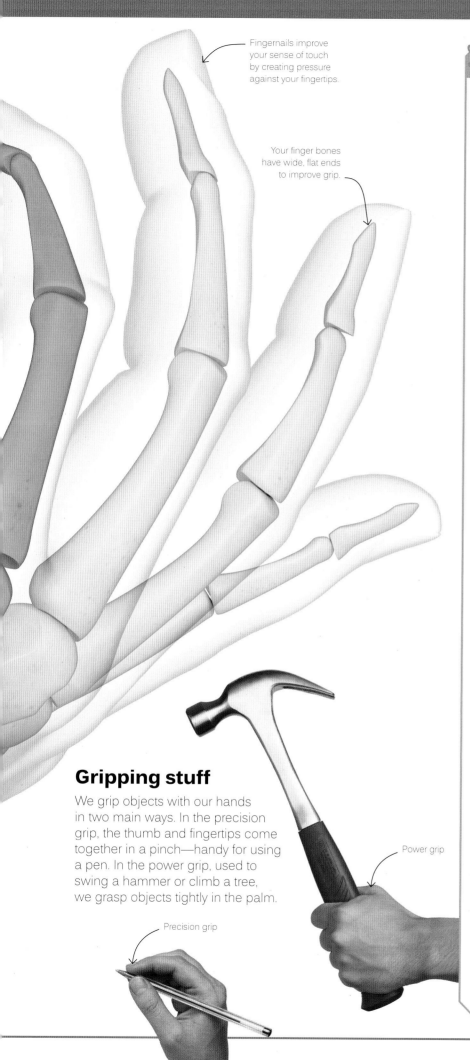

Fingernails improve your sense of touch by creating pressure against your fingertips.

Your finger bones have wide, flat ends to improve grip.

Gripping stuff

We grip objects with our hands in two main ways. In the precision grip, the thumb and fingertips come together in a pinch—handy for using a pen. In the power grip, used to swing a hammer or climb a tree, we grasp objects tightly in the palm.

Power grip

Precision grip

Opposable thumbs aren't unique to humans—lots of animals have them. But because most animals also have to use their hands as feet or as climbing tools, their thumbs work in a different way from ours.

Short thumbs

Chimpanzees have long fingers and short thumbs that suit the way they climb and hang from branches. They can't bring the thumb and fingertip together, but they can grip tools by pressing the thumb on the side of the first finger.

No thumbs

Spider monkeys have no thumbs. Instead of grasping branches, they use their fingers as hooks to hang from them. Other types of monkeys use their hands to groom each other's fur, but spider monkeys find this tricky, so they hug instead of grooming.

Double thumbs

Koalas' hands have two opposable digits rather than one, both equipped with sharp claws. This helps them grip branches more securely. Their hind feet are also unusual—the first two toes are fused to form a single toe with two claws.

TAKE A DEEP BREATH

Run your fingers down the sides of your chest. The bones you can feel are your ribs—12 pairs of long, curved bones that form a sturdy wall around your chest. Without them, your chest would collapse and your lungs wouldn't work. Your rib cage isn't a rigid frame. It has joints at the back and stretchy cartilage at the front. Together these allow your rib cage to rise and widen when you breathe.

Pump action

Your ribs play a key role in breathing, but most of the work of pumping air is done by your diaphragm. This dome-shaped sheet of muscle under the lungs pulls into a flatter shape to suck air into the lungs and then springs back into a dome to push it out again.

Breathing in

Muscles between the ribs contract, raising the ribs a little.

The diaphragm muscle pulls down forcefully.

Breathing out

Muscles between the ribs relax and the ribs drop a little.

The diaphragm springs back up, pushing air out of the lungs.

The ribs attach to a bone called the sternum (breastbone) at the front.

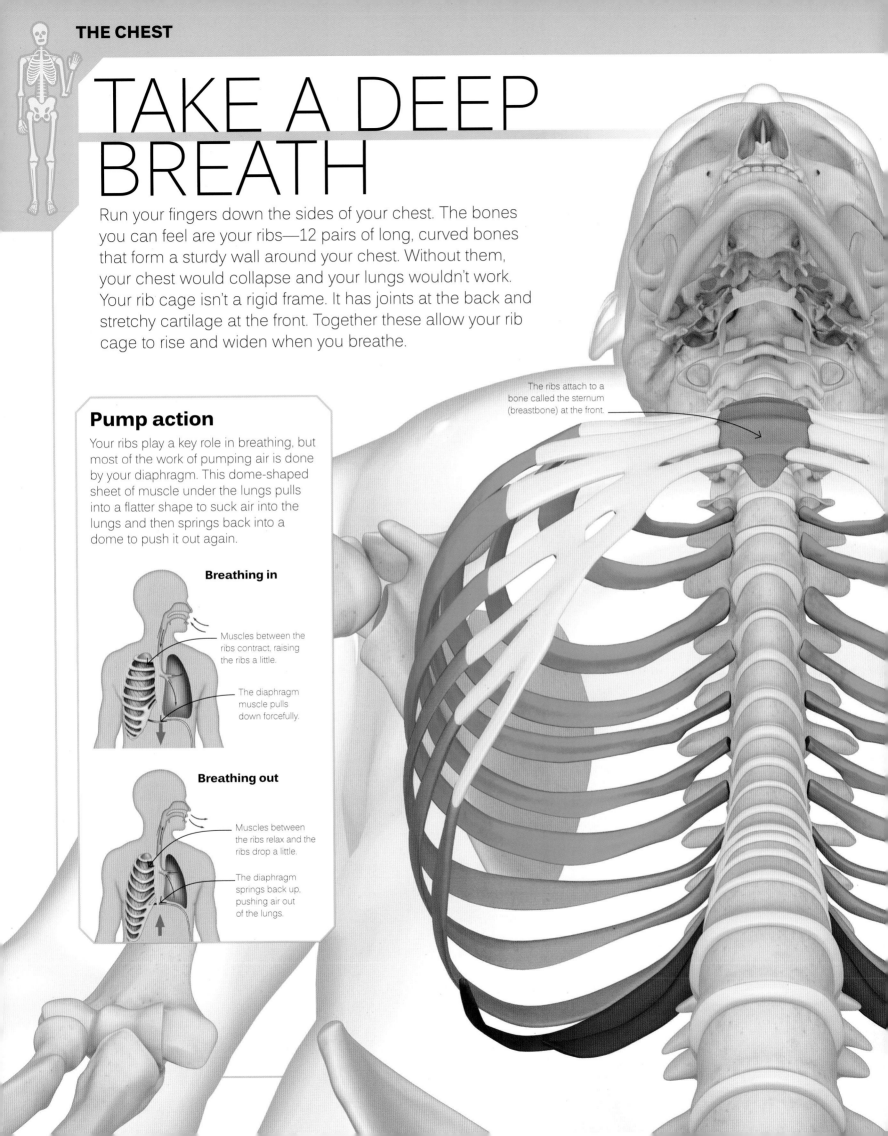

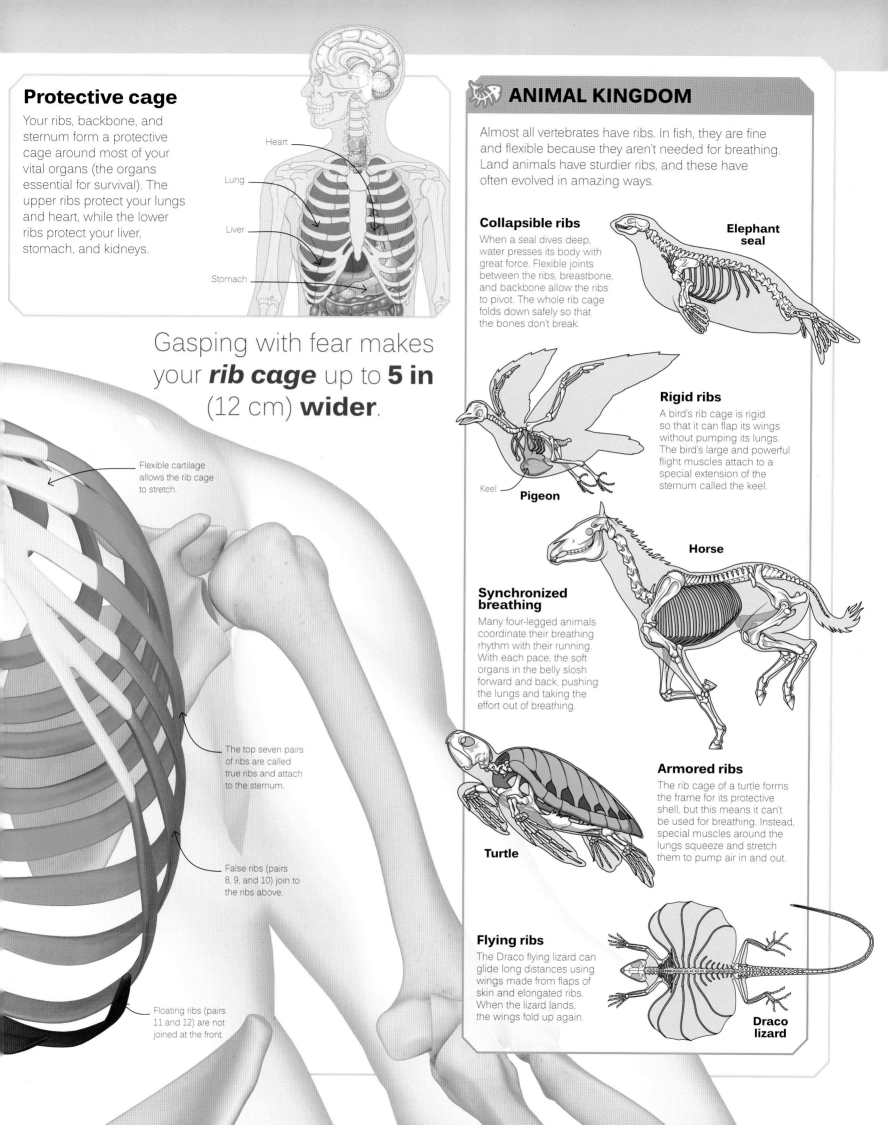

Protective cage

Your ribs, backbone, and sternum form a protective cage around most of your vital organs (the organs essential for survival). The upper ribs protect your lungs and heart, while the lower ribs protect your liver, stomach, and kidneys.

Heart

Lung

Liver

Stomach

Gasping with fear makes your *rib cage* up to **5 in** (12 cm) **wider**.

Flexible cartilage allows the rib cage to stretch.

The top seven pairs of ribs are called true ribs and attach to the sternum.

False ribs (pairs 8, 9, and 10) join to the ribs above.

Floating ribs (pairs 11 and 12) are not joined at the front.

ANIMAL KINGDOM

Almost all vertebrates have ribs. In fish, they are fine and flexible because they aren't needed for breathing. Land animals have sturdier ribs, and these have often evolved in amazing ways.

Collapsible ribs

When a seal dives deep, water presses its body with great force. Flexible joints between the ribs, breastbone, and backbone allow the ribs to pivot. The whole rib cage folds down safely so that the bones don't break.

Elephant seal

Rigid ribs

A bird's rib cage is rigid so that it can flap its wings without pumping its lungs. The bird's large and powerful flight muscles attach to a special extension of the sternum called the keel.

Keel

Pigeon

Horse

Synchronized breathing

Many four-legged animals coordinate their breathing rhythm with their running. With each pace, the soft organs in the belly slosh forward and back, pushing the lungs and taking the effort out of breathing.

Armored ribs

The rib cage of a turtle forms the frame for its protective shell, but this means it can't be used for breathing. Instead, special muscles around the lungs squeeze and stretch them to pump air in and out.

Turtle

Flying ribs

The Draco flying lizard can glide long distances using wings made from flaps of skin and elongated ribs. When the lizard lands, the wings fold up again.

Draco lizard

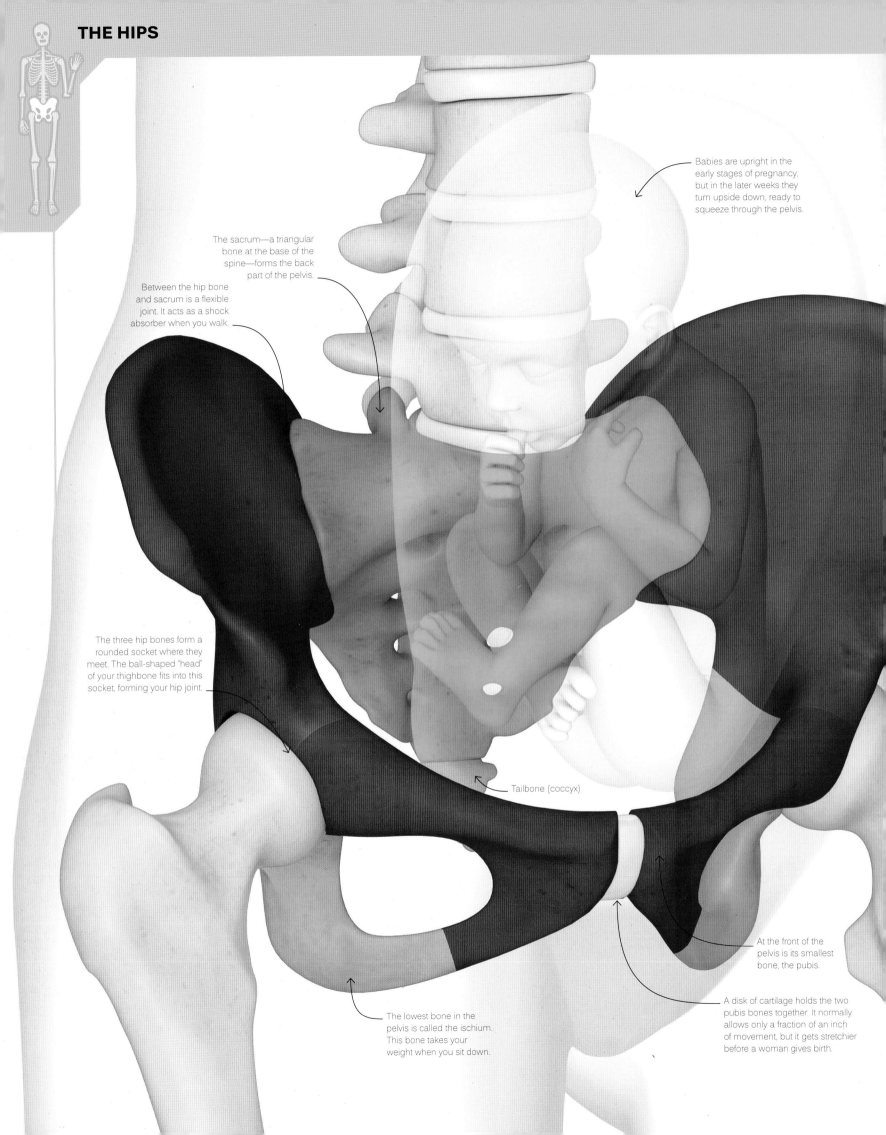

The sacrum—a triangular bone at the base of the spine—forms the back part of the pelvis.

Babies are upright in the early stages of pregnancy, but in the later weeks they turn upside down, ready to squeeze through the pelvis.

Between the hip bone and sacrum is a flexible joint. It acts as a shock absorber when you walk.

The three hip bones form a rounded socket where they meet. The ball-shaped "head" of your thighbone fits into this socket, forming your hip joint.

Tailbone (coccyx)

At the front of the pelvis is its smallest bone, the pubis.

The lowest bone in the pelvis is called the ischium. This bone takes your weight when you sit down.

A disk of cartilage holds the two pubis bones together. It normally allows only a fraction of an inch of movement, but it gets stretchier before a woman gives birth.

BONY CRADLE

Put your hands on your hips. The bones you can feel are your hip bones, which are part of your pelvis—a large and sturdy ring of bone that connects your legs to your spine. The human pelvis is large because it provides anchorage for the biggest and most powerful muscles in the body—vital for standing and walking. Its upper surface is bowl-shaped, forming a natural cradle to support the organs in your belly and the growing baby in a mother's womb.

Building the pelvis

Your pelvis is made of lots of separate bones when you're born, but most of these slowly fuse as you grow up, forming a more solid structure by your late teens. The central part, here colored turquoise, is the bottom of your spine. The two sides, each made up three bones, are your hip bones.

The largest bone in the pelvis is the ilium. Its flared top provides attachment for the muscles you need to stand and walk.

ANIMAL KINGDOM

Because the pelvis is the attachment point for an animal's rear legs, its shape reflects the way the animal walks, runs, or swims.

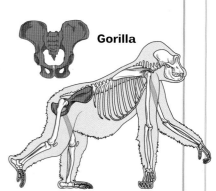

Human

Walking upright

The human pelvis has adapted to our upright style of walking and is much shorter than the pelvis of a four-legged animal. This puts the base of the spine close to the hip joints, improving stability when we're upright.

Versatile mover

A gorilla's pelvis is longer than ours and allows it to move in a variety of ways. Gorillas normally walk on all fours on the ground, but they stand to beat their chests and can even walk a few steps on two feet.

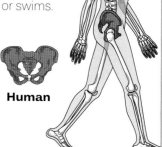

Gorilla

Almost gone

Whales lost their hind legs after adapting to life in the sea, but the pelvis didn't disappear altogether. A remnant still exists, now separate from the rest of the skeleton. It still provides an anchor point for certain muscles.

Sperm whale

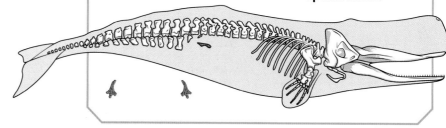

Sex difference

Women have wider hips than men because their pelvis is a different shape. When a woman gives birth, the baby must squeeze through the opening in the middle of the pelvis to leave her body—a difficult task. To make it easier, the pelvic opening is larger in women and so the whole pelvis is wider.

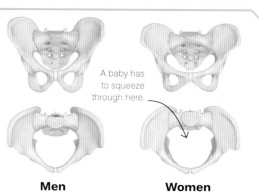

A baby has to squeeze through here.

Men   **Women**

SWINGING HIPS

Your hip joint is second in size only to your knee, yet it's one of the most mobile joints in your body. It can move in almost any direction to swing your leg forward and backward, side to side, and even twist so your knee points sideways. It's an amazing range of motion for a joint that bears forces greater than your entire weight when you walk or run. This is why human hip joints are so much larger than those of mammals that walk on four legs.

The ball is spherical, so it can turn in any direction without jamming.

Tough ligaments hold the bones in place and stop the ball from popping out of its socket.

The gluteal muscles, deep in the buttock, attach to this lever on the upper end of the thighbone.

Muscle

Ball and socket

Your hip joint's flexibility comes from its ball-and-socket design. The ball of bone at the top of the femur fits snugly into a socket in the hip bone. The inside of this joint is lined with slippery cartilage, and a lubricating liquid fills the gap. More than 20 muscles work the hip joint, including the largest muscle in the body—the gluteus maximus (buttock).

The deep socket of the hip makes it a very stable joint.

A lining of cartilage helps the bones move smoothly.

DO TRY THIS AT HOME

Test the hip joint's great range of movements for yourself. Hold on to something for safety, stand on one leg, and move the other leg in as many directions as you can. In which direction does your hip bend most—forward, backward, or to the side?

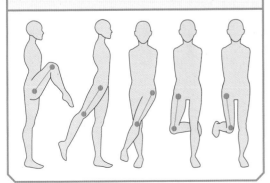

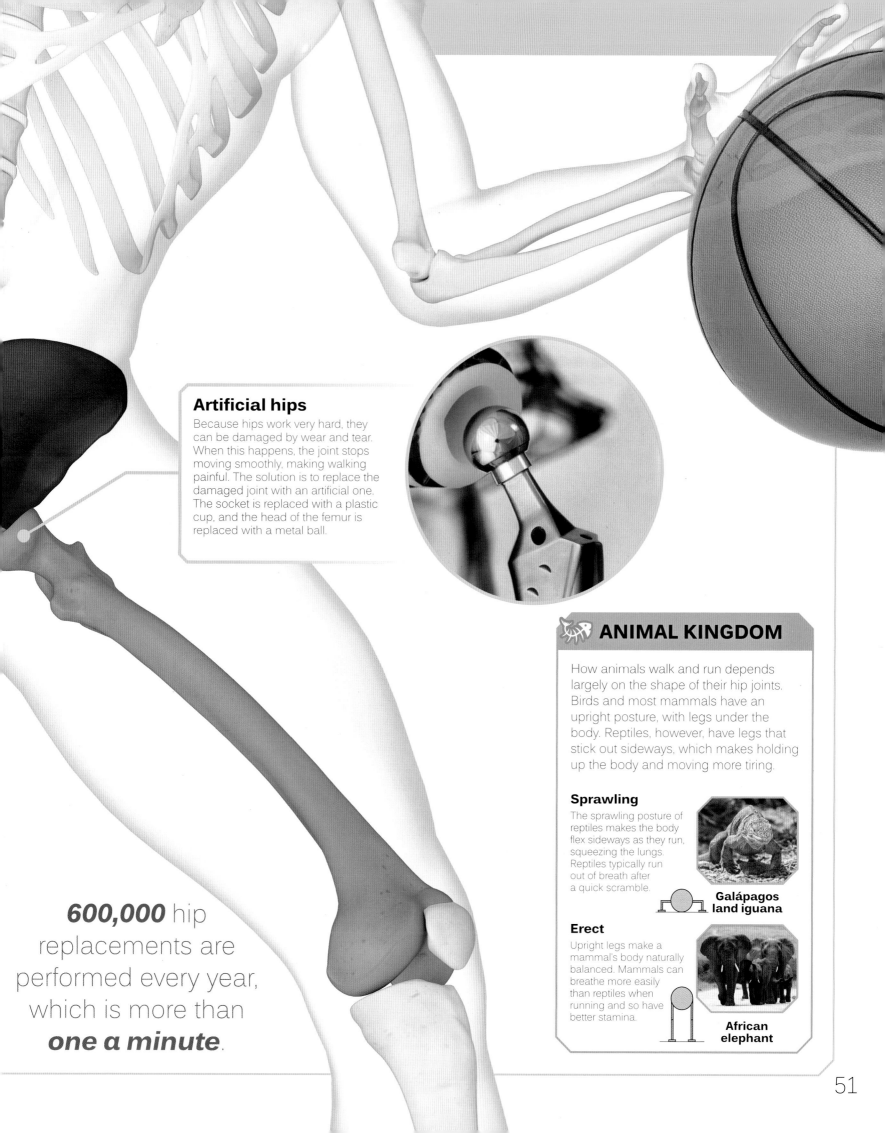

Artificial hips

Because hips work very hard, they can be damaged by wear and tear. When this happens, the joint stops moving smoothly, making walking painful. The solution is to replace the damaged joint with an artificial one. The socket is replaced with a plastic cup, and the head of the femur is replaced with a metal ball.

600,000 hip replacements are performed every year, which is more than **one a minute**.

ANIMAL KINGDOM

How animals walk and run depends largely on the shape of their hip joints. Birds and most mammals have an upright posture, with legs under the body. Reptiles, however, have legs that stick out sideways, which makes holding up the body and moving more tiring.

Sprawling

The sprawling posture of reptiles makes the body flex sideways as they run, squeezing the lungs. Reptiles typically run out of breath after a quick scramble.

Galápagos land iguana

Erect

Upright legs make a mammal's body naturally balanced. Mammals can breathe more easily than reptiles when running and so have better stamina.

African elephant

Out of the trees

Walking upright on two legs is a strange way for a mammal to get around, but our close relatives, the great apes, often stand on two legs in trees while holding on with their hands. When our ancestors left the trees around 5 million years ago, walking on two legs may have come naturally. Since then, the shape of the skeleton has changed to make walking and running easier and faster.

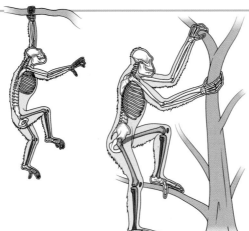

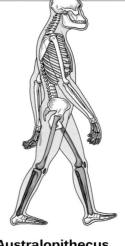

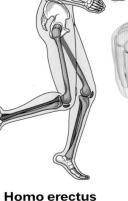

Oreopithecus

Our species evolved from apes like *Oreopithecus*, which lived about 8 million years ago. *Oreopithecus* had an upright posture when climbing and swinging in trees.

Ardipithecus

Ardipithecus lived 4.4 million years ago. Like a chimp, it had long arms and grasping toes. Its mid-foot, however, was rigid, meaning that it could stand and walk upright.

Australopithecus

Footprints left by this ape 3.7 million years ago prove it could walk on two feet. However, it had large, powerful arms and could probably climb trees quickly to escape danger.

Homo erectus

Our direct ancestor, *Homo erectus* appeared 1.9 million years ago and had the tall, athletic build of a modern human, though its brain was the size of a 1-year-old's.

BORN TO RUN

A newborn horse can walk within an hour of birth, but a human baby takes a year to learn to walk. Walking is easier for a four-legged animal because its body has a wide base and a low center of gravity. Our vertical skeleton, with only two legs to support it, is less stable. For us, walking is a balancing act that involves the coordination of hundreds of muscles—not just in the legs but also in the hips, back, shoulders, arms, and neck. Each step forward is a controlled fall, with the legs repeatedly swinging forward to stop us from tipping over.

Long legs

Our legs contain the largest and strongest bones and joints in the body, and are built to withstand powerful forces that pass through our skeletons when we move. Our leg bones are much longer than those of relatives such as chimpanzees and gorillas. Longer bones give a longer stride, which means a faster walking and running speed.

Kneecap

Top speeds

Despite our long legs, we're very slow runners compared to many four-legged mammals. Even a cat can outpace human athletes over a short sprint. However, we are built for endurance and can jog great distances in hot weather without overheating as much as other animals.

Cheetah
Pronghorn
Springbok
Lion
Hare
Greyhound
Kangaroo
Horse
Tiger
Black Rhino
Human
Elephant

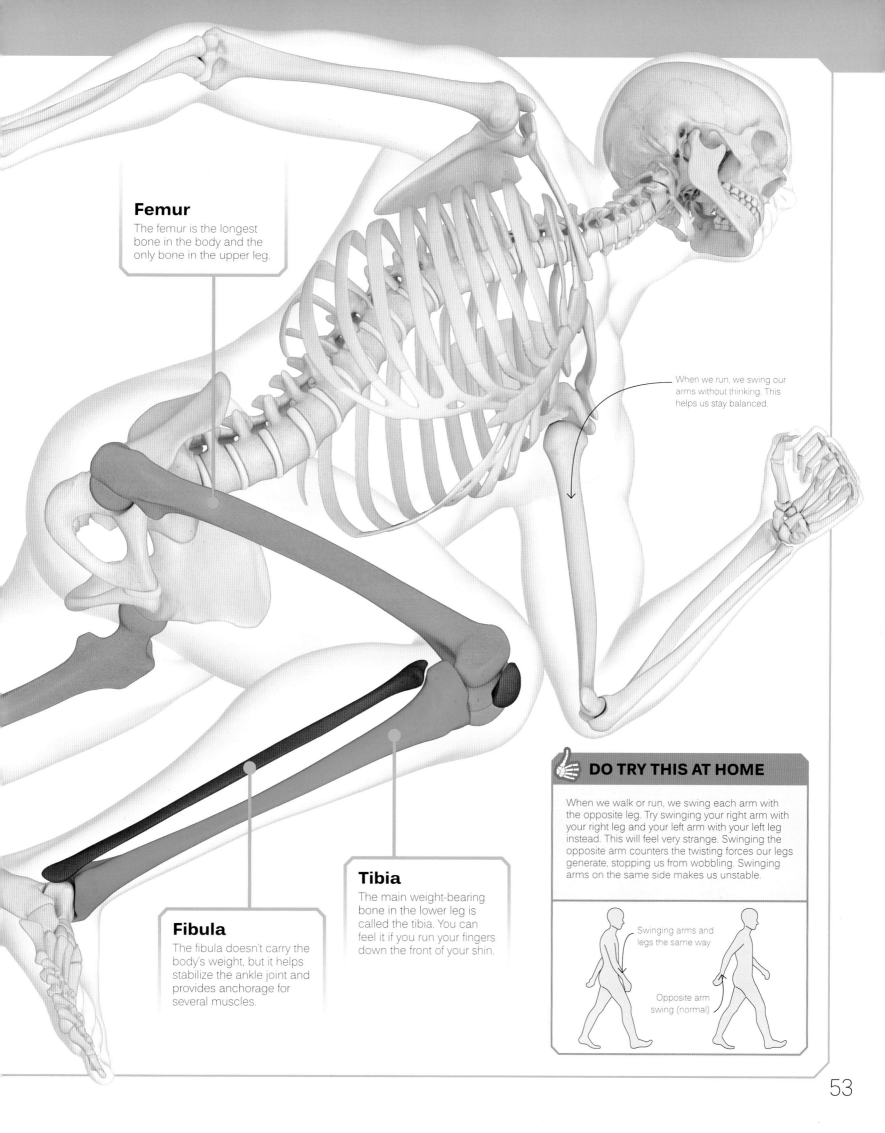

Femur

The femur is the longest bone in the body and the only bone in the upper leg.

When we run, we swing our arms without thinking. This helps us stay balanced.

Fibula

The fibula doesn't carry the body's weight, but it helps stabilize the ankle joint and provides anchorage for several muscles.

Tibia

The main weight-bearing bone in the lower leg is called the tibia. You can feel it if you run your fingers down the front of your shin.

👆 DO TRY THIS AT HOME

When we walk or run, we swing each arm with the opposite leg. Try swinging your right arm with your right leg and your left arm with your left leg instead. This will feel very strange. Swinging the opposite arm counters the twisting forces our legs generate, stopping us from wobbling. Swinging arms on the same side makes us unstable.

Swinging arms and legs the same way

Opposite arm swing (normal)

LONGEST AND STRONGEST

The bones in your skeleton have to carry more than just your body weight. When you walk, forces equal to twice your weight pass through your legs with each stride, and when you run or jump, the forces can exceed ten times your weight. Your femurs—the only bones in your thighs— are built to withstand this stress. The longest and strongest bones in the body, they can support up to 6 tons each before breaking— about the weight of four cars.

Pillar of strength

The tremendous strength of the femur comes largely from its internal structure. The main shaft is a cylinder—a shape that can support great loads. Its wall is made of compact bone and is thickest in the middle to resist bending. The ends are braced internally by crisscrossing struts of spongy bone, which is strong yet lightweight.

The main shaft is a cylinder of compact bone. The hollow in the middle is used to store fat.

The lower end of the femur forms part of the knee—the largest joint in the body.

The small hollows in the ends of the femur contain bone marrow, which makes blood cells.

Walk this way

One of the reasons we can stand and walk more easily than apes is that our femurs slope inward from hip to knee. This keeps our legs and feet directly under the body, carrying our weight. Ape femurs, in contrast, are vertical when they stand. To stay upright, they rely on muscle power and must use four times more energy when walking than we do. The awkward posture also makes them rock sideways with each step.

The human hip, knee, and ankle joint form a straight line.

Chimps have a wide stance that is tiring to maintain.

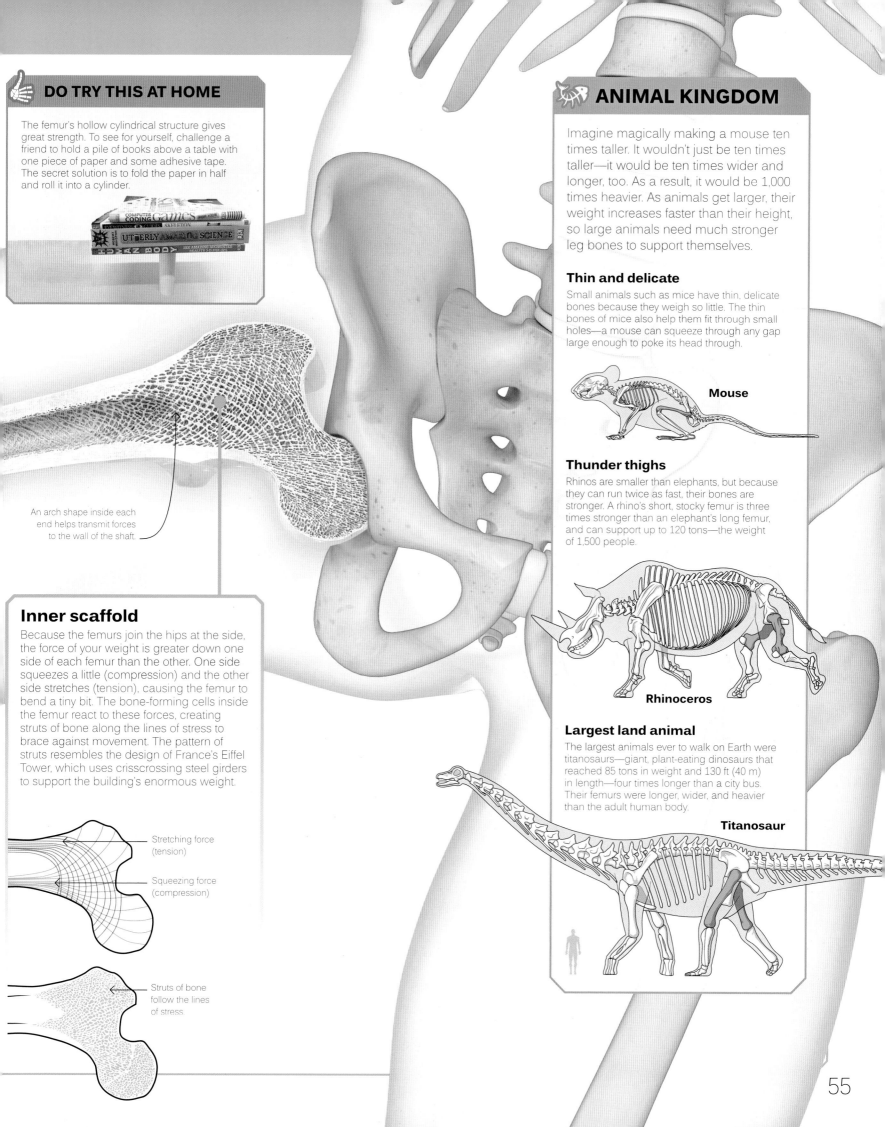

The femur's hollow cylindrical structure gives great strength. To see for yourself, challenge a friend to hold a pile of books above a table with one piece of paper and some adhesive tape. The secret solution is to fold the paper in half and roll it into a cylinder.

An arch shape inside each end helps transmit forces to the wall of the shaft.

Inner scaffold

Because the femurs join the hips at the side, the force of your weight is greater down one side of each femur than the other. One side squeezes a little (compression) and the other side stretches (tension), causing the femur to bend a tiny bit. The bone-forming cells inside the femur react to these forces, creating struts of bone along the lines of stress to brace against movement. The pattern of struts resembles the design of France's Eiffel Tower, which uses crisscrossing steel girders to support the building's enormous weight.

Stretching force (tension)

Squeezing force (compression)

Struts of bone follow the lines of stress.

Imagine magically making a mouse ten times taller. It wouldn't just be ten times taller—it would be ten times wider and longer, too. As a result, it would be 1,000 times heavier. As animals get larger, their weight increases faster than their height, so large animals need much stronger leg bones to support themselves.

Thin and delicate

Small animals such as mice have thin, delicate bones because they weigh so little. The thin bones of mice also help them fit through small holes—a mouse can squeeze through any gap large enough to poke its head through.

Mouse

Thunder thighs

Rhinos are smaller than elephants, but because they can run twice as fast, their bones are stronger. A rhino's short, stocky femur is three times stronger than an elephant's long femur, and can support up to 120 tons—the weight of 1,500 people.

Rhinoceros

Largest land animal

The largest animals ever to walk on Earth were titanosaurs—giant, plant-eating dinosaurs that reached 85 tons in weight and 130 ft (40 m) in length—four times longer than a city bus. Their femurs were longer, wider, and heavier than the adult human body.

Titanosaur

BENDED KNEES

To see just how important the knee joint is, try walking or jumping without bending your legs. The knee is the largest joint in the body and carries all your weight when you move. Flexed by the powerful muscles of the thigh, it propels you forward as you walk or run, but it can also lock in a vertical position so you can stand still without tiring. To make best use of muscle power, the knee is restricted to move in only one direction, like a hinge, though it can rotate a little too. A complex system of ligaments stabilizes its hingelike movement, but these also make it prone to twisting injuries.

Inside the knee

Four bones, 12 muscles, and over 10 ligaments meet in the knee, making it the body's most complex joint. Unlike the hip, the knee doesn't have a deep socket to hold the bones in place. Instead, the ends of the thighbone and shinbone slide around each other, held in place by muscles, tendons, and ligaments.

A groove in the end of the femur stops the kneecap from slipping out.

Thighbone (femur)

Kneecap (patella)

The ends of the femur and tibia are coated in slippery cartilage to help the joint move smoothly.

Shinbone (tibia)

Calf bone (fibula)

Lever action

The knobby bone on the front of your knee is the kneecap, or patella. This small bone is embedded in the tendon that pulls your shin to straighten your leg. By increasing the space between the femur and the tendon, it gives the joint extra leverage, making it easier to straighten the leg.

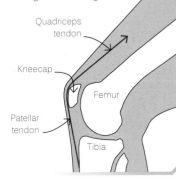

Quadriceps tendon

Kneecap

Patellar tendon

Femur

Tibia

DO TRY THIS AT HOME

Ask a friend to sit so their legs are free to swing. Then, when they least expect it, tap the skin below a kneecap. If you do it right, the leg will twitch. This is the knee-jerk reflex and it happens without thinking because the nerve signal takes a shortcut that avoids the brain. The reflex helps you stay balanced while standing by keeping the tendon below the kneecap tight.

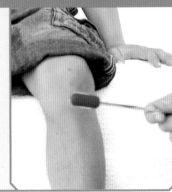

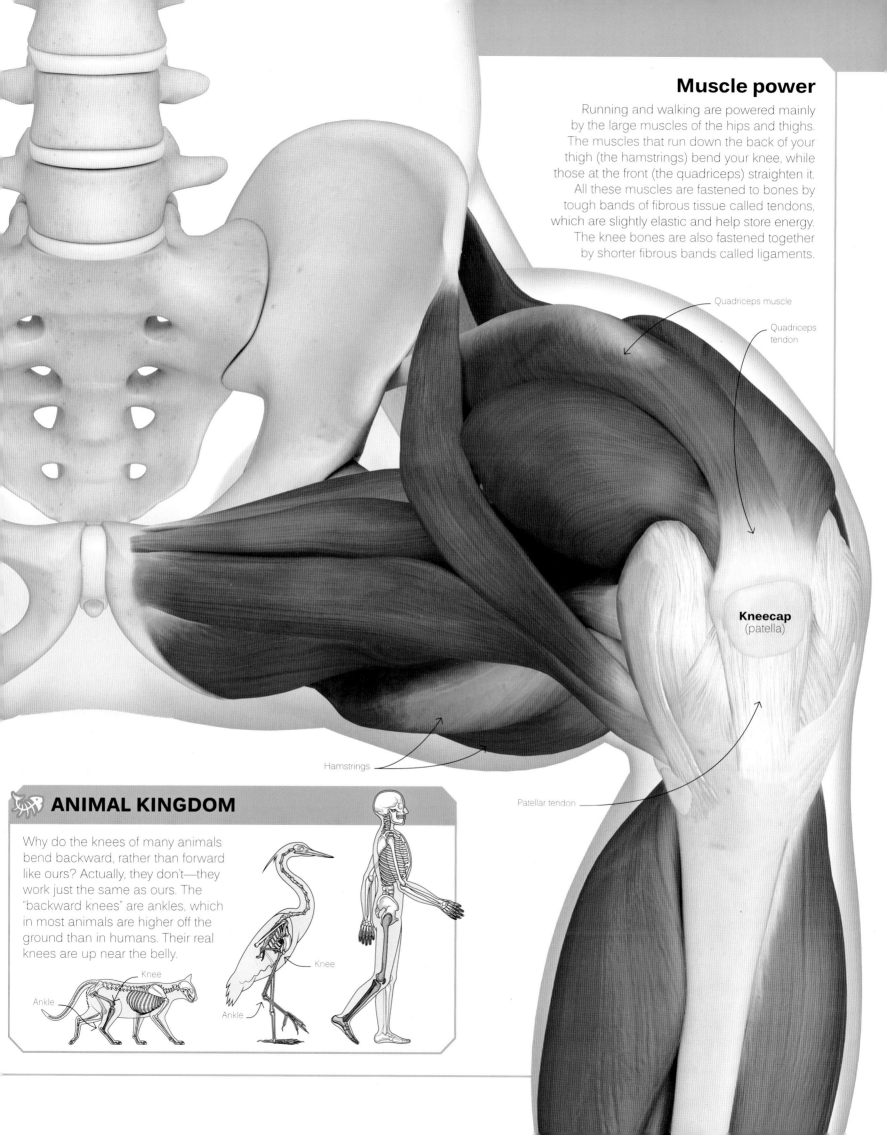

Muscle power

Running and walking are powered mainly by the large muscles of the hips and thighs. The muscles that run down the back of your thigh (the hamstrings) bend your knee, while those at the front (the quadriceps) straighten it. All these muscles are fastened to bones by tough bands of fibrous tissue called tendons, which are slightly elastic and help store energy. The knee bones are also fastened together by shorter fibrous bands called ligaments.

Quadriceps muscle

Quadriceps tendon

Kneecap
(patella)

Hamstrings

Patellar tendon

ANIMAL KINGDOM

Why do the knees of many animals bend backward, rather than forward like ours? Actually, they don't—they work just the same as ours. The "backward knees" are ankles, which in most animals are higher off the ground than in humans. Their real knees are up near the belly.

Knee

Ankle

Knee

Ankle

FEET FIRST

Your feet are built like your hands, but the 26 bones in each foot are shaped to form a stable platform to carry your weight. When you walk, your feet lift your whole body, tipping your body into a fall on each step and then catching you again. If you live to be 80, your feet will take about 220 million steps in your lifetime, carrying you a distance of 110,000 miles (177,000 km)—nearly three times around the world.

ANIMAL KINGDOM

Humans are unusual in walking on only two feet, but we aren't the only vertebrates to do it. This is how a few other species get around on half the usual number of limbs.

Hopping

Kangaroos are the only large animals that move by hopping. Stretchy tendons in their legs store energy with each landing, releasing it as they spring back up. Large tails keep them balanced.

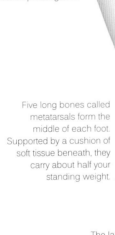

Water walking

In an emergency, the Jesus lizard rears up on its hind legs for extra speed. Its wide feet scamper so fast that it can run across the surface of water.

Sprinting

The fastest animal on two feet is the ostrich, which can reach speeds of up to 45 mph (75 km/h). Its long legs give it a huge stride, and its elastic leg tendons store twice as much energy as those in our legs.

Jumping sideways

The sifaka's long legs are great for jumping through trees but not for running on all fours. It moves over open ground by leaping sideways, arms outstretched for balance.

Each of your feet has 14 toe bones, called phalanges.

Five long bones called metatarsals form the middle of each foot. Supported by a cushion of soft tissue beneath, they carry about half your standing weight.

The largest bone in your foot is your heel bone, or calcaneus. When you walk, it takes all your weight as you put your foot down.

DO TRY THIS AT HOME

Try making footprints on the bathroom floor with wet feet. Because your feet are arched, you'll see a large gap in the middle. You can also see that the main contact points between your feet and the ground form a triangle—a shape that gives extra stability.

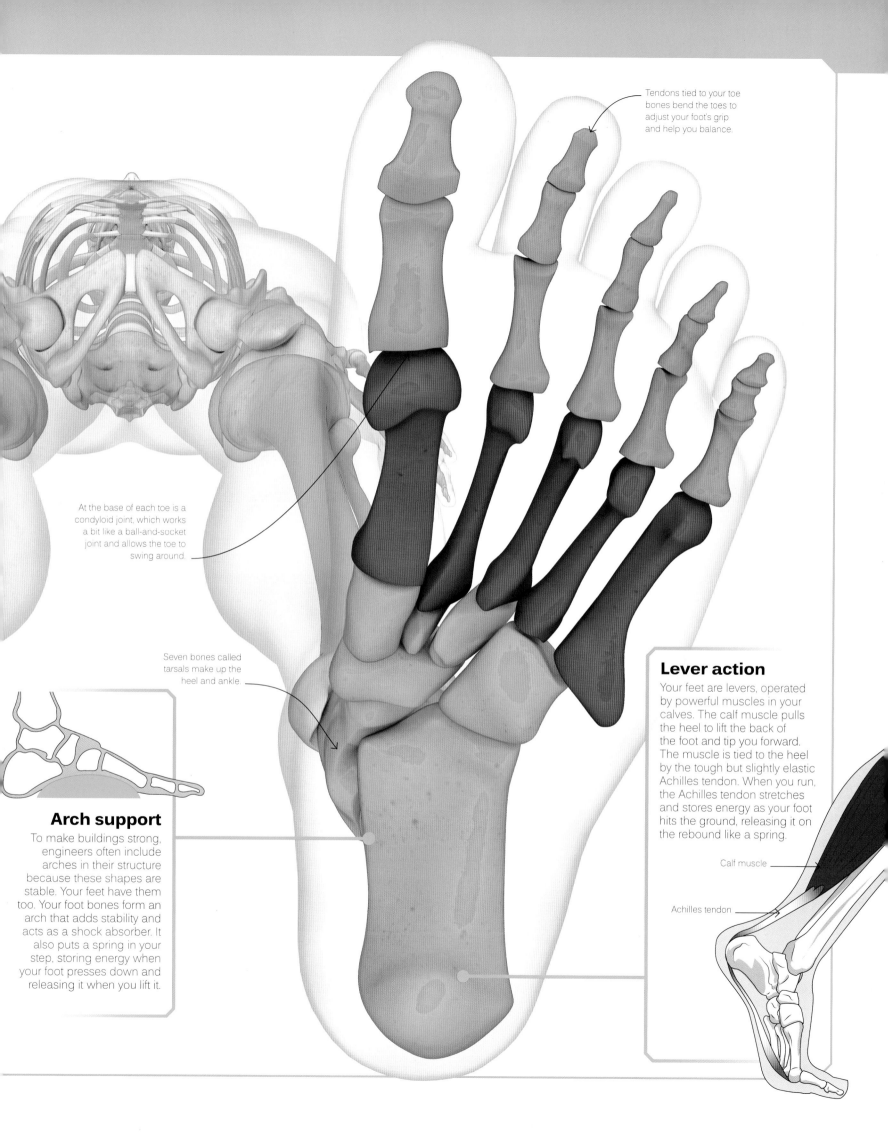

Tendons tied to your toe bones bend the toes to adjust your foot's grip and help you balance.

At the base of each toe is a condyloid joint, which works a bit like a ball-and-socket joint and allows the toe to swing around.

Seven bones called tarsals make up the heel and ankle.

Lever action

Your feet are levers, operated by powerful muscles in your calves. The calf muscle pulls the heel to lift the back of the foot and tip you forward. The muscle is tied to the heel by the tough but slightly elastic Achilles tendon. When you run, the Achilles tendon stretches and stores energy as your foot hits the ground, releasing it on the rebound like a spring.

Calf muscle

Achilles tendon

Arch support

To make buildings strong, engineers often include arches in their structure because these shapes are stable. Your feet have them too. Your foot bones form an arch that adds stability and acts as a shock absorber. It also puts a spring in your step, storing energy when your foot presses down and releasing it when you lift it.

ON YOUR TOES

Hidden away inside socks and shoes, your toes might seem like the least important part of your body, but they are very important. To see why, take off your shoes and try walking without touching the ground with your toes. When you walk normally, your toes carry the weight of your whole body at the end of each stride, and they give the final push that propels your body forward.

 ANIMAL KINGDOM

Different vertebrates use different bones to make contact with the ground when they walk or run. The fastest are those that touch their ground only with their toes. The different styles of moving are known as plantigrade, digitigrade, and unguligrade.

Plantigrade

Plantigrade animals, such as bears and humans, walk with their toes and metatarsals flat. This style of walking is slow, but larger feet carry weight well and make the body stable.

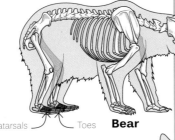

Metatarsals   Toes   **Bear**

Digitigrade

Dog, cats, and most birds walk on their toes, with their heels raised. This gives them a longer stride, making them fast, and their small feet allow them to move quietly.

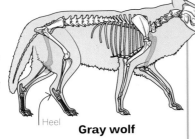

Heel   **Gray wolf**

Unguligrade

Hoofed mammals walk on the very tips of their toes, which are capped with hooves. Horses have only a single toe in each foot. Such animals are built for speed—running is their first line of defense when predators attack.

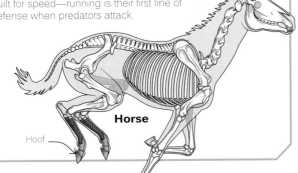

Horse

Hoof

Walking only on the toes, which is how cats move, makes your footsteps much quieter.

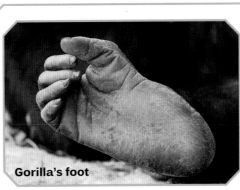

Gorilla's foot

Handy toes

Most apes have long toes for gripping branches. Their big toes are opposable, like thumbs, letting their feet work the same way as hands. Our ancestors had feet like these, but they changed to become stable platforms for walking after we left the trees.

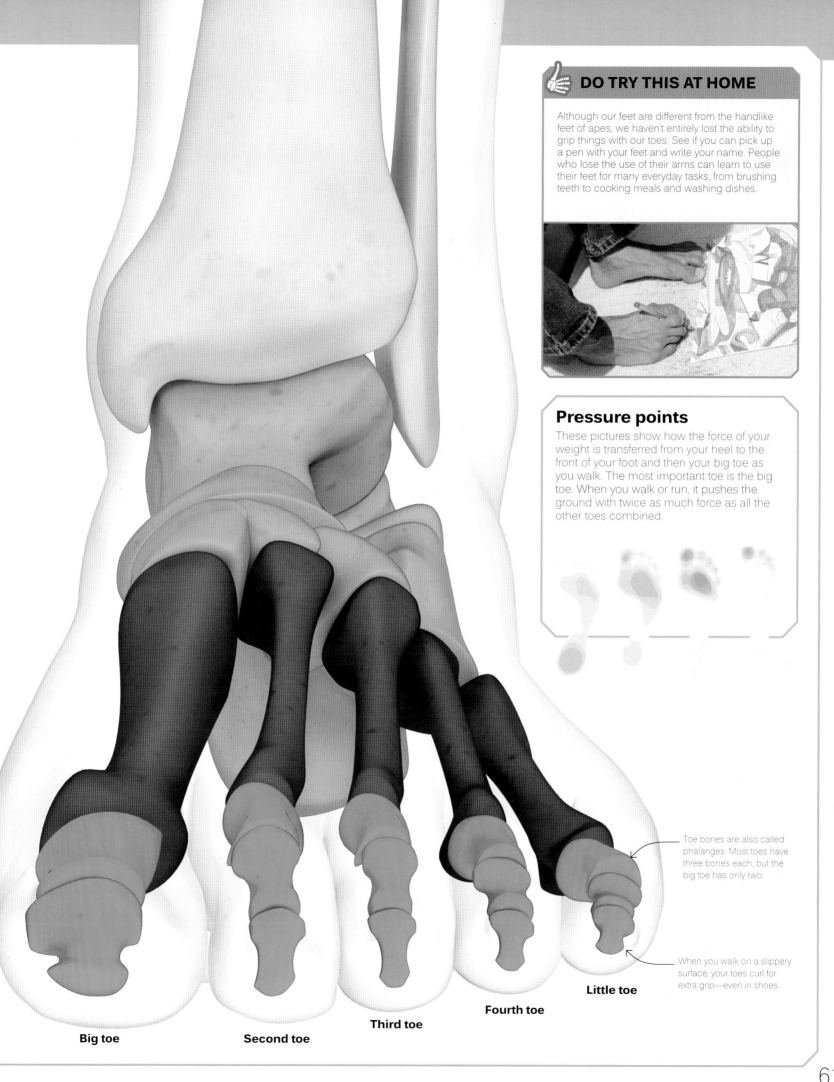

![thumb icon] **DO TRY THIS AT HOME**

Although our feet are different from the handlike feet of apes, we haven't entirely lost the ability to grip things with our toes. See if you can pick up a pen with your feet and write your name. People who lose the use of their arms can learn to use their feet for many everyday tasks, from brushing teeth to cooking meals and washing dishes.

Pressure points

These pictures show how the force of your weight is transferred from your heel to the front of your foot and then your big toe as you walk. The most important toe is the big toe. When you walk or run, it pushes the ground with twice as much force as all the other toes combined.

Toe bones are also called phalanges. Most toes have three bones each, but the big toe has only two.

When you walk on a slippery surface, your toes curl for extra grip—even in shoes.

Little toe

Fourth toe

Third toe

Big toe

Second toe

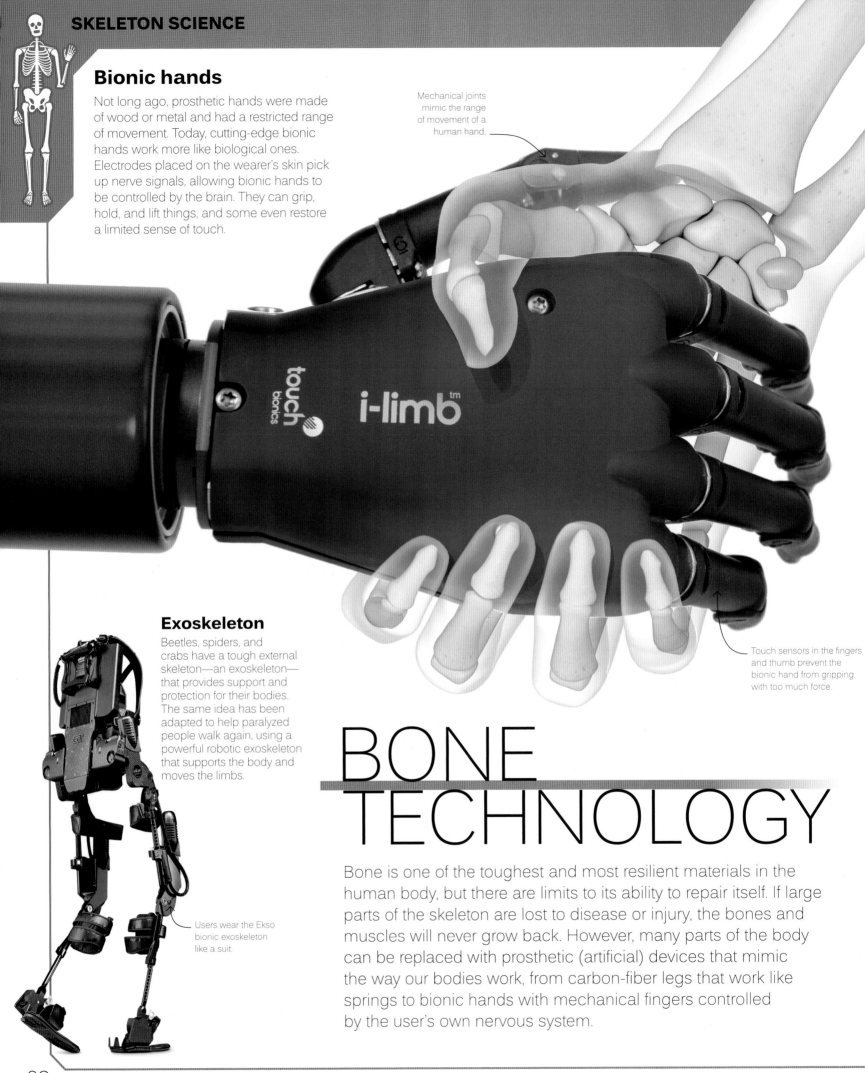

Bionic hands

Not long ago, prosthetic hands were made of wood or metal and had a restricted range of movement. Today, cutting-edge bionic hands work more like biological ones. Electrodes placed on the wearer's skin pick up nerve signals, allowing bionic hands to be controlled by the brain. They can grip, hold, and lift things, and some even restore a limited sense of touch.

Mechanical joints mimic the range of movement of a human hand.

touch bionics

i-limb™

Touch sensors in the fingers and thumb prevent the bionic hand from gripping with too much force.

Exoskeleton

Beetles, spiders, and crabs have a tough external skeleton—an exoskeleton— that provides support and protection for their bodies. The same idea has been adapted to help paralyzed people walk again, using a powerful robotic exoskeleton that supports the body and moves the limbs.

Users wear the Ekso bionic exoskeleton like a suit.

BONE TECHNOLOGY

Bone is one of the toughest and most resilient materials in the human body, but there are limits to its ability to repair itself. If large parts of the skeleton are lost to disease or injury, the bones and muscles will never grow back. However, many parts of the body can be replaced with prosthetic (artificial) devices that mimic the way our bodies work, from carbon-fiber legs that work like springs to bionic hands with mechanical fingers controlled by the user's own nervous system.

Artificial bone

Doctors can now use artificial materials not only to bridge gaps but also to act as scaffolds for growing new bone tissue. Ceramics based on calcium phosphate (the mineral found in bone) contain tiny pores that can be seeded with bone cells collected from a person's marrow. Over time, the cells create new bone tissue that fuses with the ceramic implant.

Lifelike prosthetic hands are shaped and colored to match the wearer.

This ceramic implant was made to replace the end of a damaged bone.

This implant has been shaped to fit a hole in a 3-D printed model of a patient's skull.

Skin deep

Some prosthetic limbs are remarkably lifelike. Made of rubberlike silicone, they are hand-painted to match the user's skin and can be given freckles, hairs, and tattoos. Unlike mechanical devices, lifelike hands offer only a limited range of functions, such as pushing, pulling, and typing.

3-D printing

Large gaps in bones can be repaired with implants made from inorganic materials, such as titanium or ceramic. These work best when they fit perfectly, allowing the implant to bond to the bone. To ensure a precise fit, doctors can use scanning machines to map the existing bone and 3-D printers to shape a matching implant.

Scanning machines

Doctors use scanning machines to see detailed 3-D images of the skeleton inside a patient's body. CT (computed tomography) scanners use X-ray cameras to take lots of pictures from different angles and then combine them on a computer to make a 3-D model. MRI (magnetic resonance imaging) scanners work in a similar way but use powerful magnets to make hydrogen atoms in soft tissues emit radio waves, which are then used to construct an image.

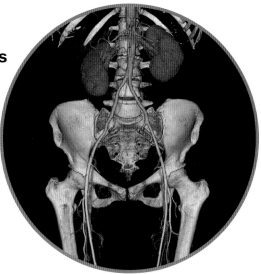

Running strong

Bladelike prosthetic legs made of reinforced plastic or carbon fiber have been developed for disabled athletes. These flex as they press the ground and then spring back into shape, giving a push that makes running faster and more efficient. Athletes using these legs are fast enough to compete with able-bodied competitors.

BONE DETECTIVES

After death, the soft tissues of the body soon decay and disappear. Bones and teeth, however, are harder and can last hundreds or even thousands of years. Ancient skeletons provide a fascinating window into the past. The scientists who study them are called forensic archaeologists and work like detectives at a crime scene, searching for clues that might reveal who a person was, how they lived and died, and even what they ate.

Buried treasure

The objects buried with a skeleton can be as interesting as the bones. The skeleton above was buried in Bulgaria 4,500 years ago with 990 gold objects. Such precious objects suggest a person was wealthy or powerful.

The number of teeth and the amount of dental wear reveal how old a person was and what they ate.

The clavicle (collarbone) is the last bone to finish growing and helps reveal the person's age.

The shape of the pelvis shows whether a skeleton is male or female.

Artificial eyes made of colored glass were placed in this Egyptian mummy's eye sockets.

Mummified body

The ancient Egyptians mummified people after death. Soft organs were removed and the body was filled with salt to dry it out. After drying, it was wrapped in linen and placed in a tomb with valuable objects. This mummy was a priest's daughter named Tamut. She died in her 30s about 1,100 years ago.

Some bones may show signs of disease or injury. This mummy's jaw had a hole caused by severe tooth decay.

Arm bones can reveal how much exercise a person got. Very sturdy bones suggest a life of hard labor—common in slaves.

Damaged bones reveal injuries. A major injury that doesn't show signs of healing is a possible cause of death.

Rebuilding the past

Forensic scientists can rebuild the faces of dead people from skulls by using clay to mimic facial muscles. This can also be done to reveal what our distant ancestors might have looked like. These pictures show the reconstruction of *Homo habilis*—a prehistoric species that may have been an ancestor of modern humans.

Studying the skull

The sculptor studies the skull and looks for rough patches on the bone. These show where muscles attached and give clues to how thick they were.

Adding pegs

Next he adds pegs to show how deep the overlying flesh was. Muscles and skin will be thin over the forehead and thick over the cheeks.

Adding flesh

The sculptor uses layers of modeling clay to rebuild the flesh. The shape of the nasal opening helps him figure out the size and shape of the nose.

Finishing touches

Next he paints the face with lifelike colors. He adds glass eyes and carefully inserts individual hairs into the scalp.

Fascinating fossils

Buried bones don't last forever, but their shapes can be preserved for millions of years by fossils. Fossils form when water seeping through the ground replaces organic remains with rock minerals. This fossilized *Homo habilis* skull is 2 million years old and was carefully pieced together from fragments.

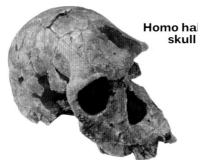

Homo habilis skull

Chemical clues

Some skeletons only give up their secrets in a laboratory. Here, scientists cut open the bones and analyze the chemicals trapped inside.

Carbon dating

Scientists can work out the exact age of bones by measuring the level of carbon-14—a natural form of the element carbon. This process works because after a person dies, the percentage of carbon-14 in their body halves every 5,700 years.

DNA testing

A person's genes are stored as a unique code in the molecule DNA. Scientists can extract DNA from bone and use the code to figure out who a person's living relatives are.

Food and diet

By measuring the level of different variants of the element nitrogen in bones, scientists can tell whether a person ate lots of meat and dairy food—a sign of wealth— or got most of their protein from bread and plant food.

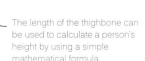

The length of the thighbone can be used to calculate a person's height by using a simple mathematical formula.

Plates of gold or metal were placed on Tamut's toenails and fingernails.

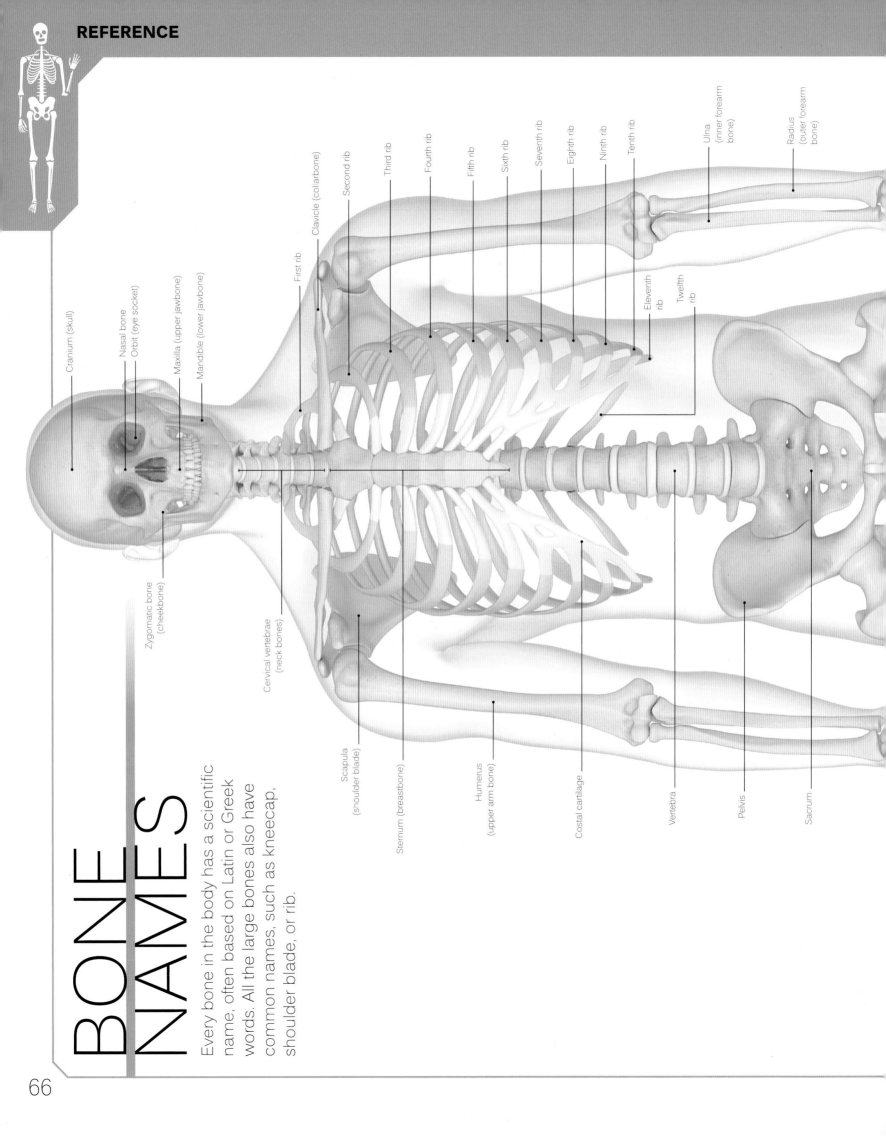

BONE NAMES

Every bone in the body has a scientific name, often based on Latin or Greek words. All the large bones also have common names, such as kneecap, shoulder blade, or rib.

Cranium (skull)

Nasal bone

Orbit (eye socket)

Maxilla (upper jawbone)

Mandible (lower jawbone)

Zygomatic bone (cheekbone)

Cervical vertebrae (neck bones)

Scapula (shoulder blade)

Sternum (breastbone)

Humerus (upper arm bone)

Costal cartilage

Vertebra

Pelvis

Sacrum

First rib

Clavicle (collarbone)

Second rib

Third rib

Fourth rib

Fifth rib

Sixth rib

Seventh rib

Eighth rib

Ninth rib

Tenth rib

Eleventh rib

Twelfth rib

Ulna (inner forearm bone)

Radius (outer forearm bone)

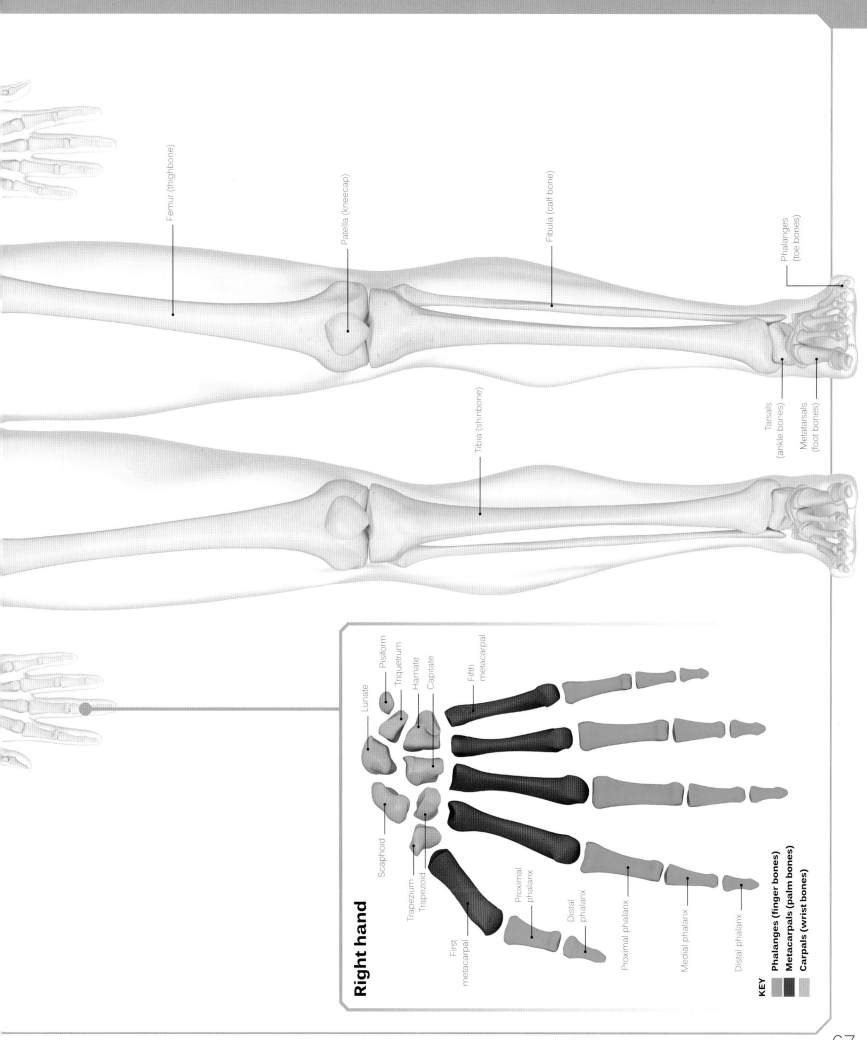

Femur (thighbone)

Patella (kneecap)

Fibula (calf bone)

Tibia (shinbone)

Phalanges (toe bones)

Tarsals (ankle bones)

Metatarsals (foot bones)

Right hand

Lunate

Pisiform

Triquetrum

Hamate

Capitate

Fifth metacarpal

Scaphoid

Trapezium

Trapezoid

First metacarpal

Proximal phalanx

Distal phalanx

Proximal phalanx

Medial phalanx

Distal phalanx

KEY
- Phalanges (finger bones)
- Metacarpals (palm bones)
- Carpals (wrist bones)

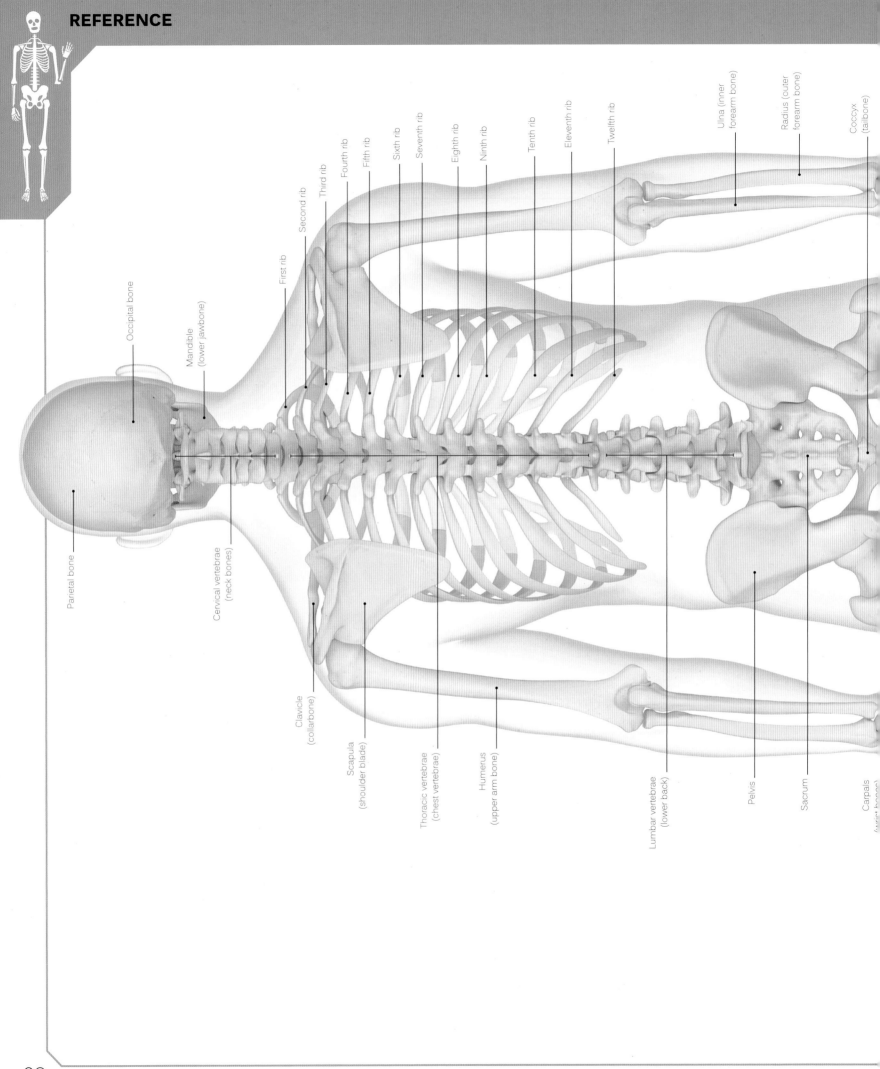

Occipital bone

Mandible
(lower jawbone)

First rib

Second rib

Third rib

Fourth rib

Fifth rib

Sixth rib

Seventh rib

Eighth rib

Ninth rib

Tenth rib

Eleventh rib

Twelfth rib

Ulna (inner
forearm bone)

Radius (outer
forearm bone)

Coccyx
(tailbone)

Parietal bone

Cervical vertebrae
(neck bones)

Clavicle
(collarbone)

Scapula
(shoulder blade)

Thoracic vertebrae
(chest vertebrae)

Humerus
(upper arm bone)

Lumbar vertebrae
(lower back)

Pelvis

Sacrum

Carpals
(wrist bones)

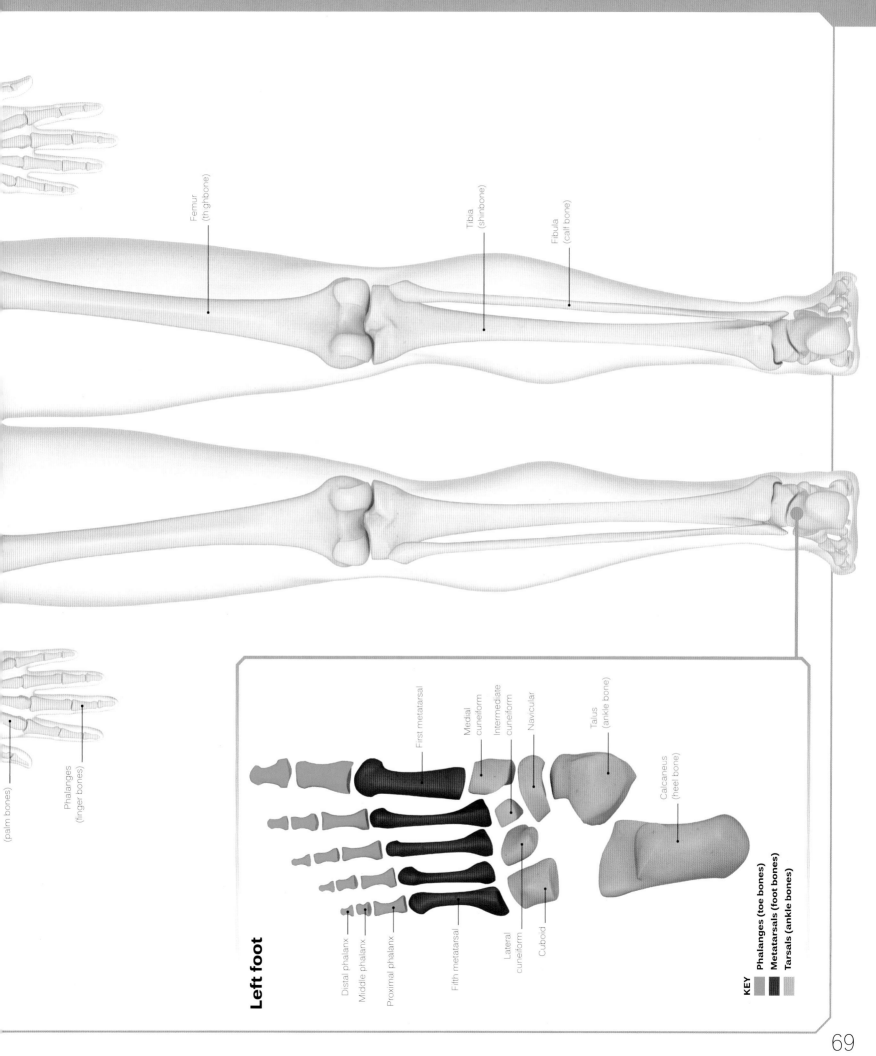

Femur (thighbone)

Tibia (shinbone)

Fibula (calf bone)

(palm bones)

Phalanges (finger bones)

Left foot

Distal phalanx

Middle phalanx

Proximal phalanx

Fifth metatarsal

First metatarsal

Medial cuneiform

Intermediate cuneiform

Navicular

Talus (ankle bone)

Calcaneus (heel bone)

Lateral cuneiform

Cuboid

KEY

Phalanges (toe bones)

Metatarsals (foot bones)

Tarsals (ankle bones)

GLOSSARY

abdomen
The belly or lower part of the main body, below the chest.

antagonistic muscles
Muscles that pull in opposite directions, with one member of the pair pulling the bone one way, and the other pulling it back.

blood
A liquid that is the body's main transportation substance. It carries oxygen, nutrients, minerals, hormones, vitamins, and various cells, as well as collecting waste chemicals for disposal. The red color of blood comes from the oxygen-carrying pigment hemoglobin inside blood cells.

blood vessel
A tube through which blood flows.

bone marrow
A soft tissue that fills the cavities inside bone and makes blood cells or stores fat.

callus
A rounded structure that forms around a fracture while a bone is healing. A soft callus is made of cartilage, but a hard callus is made of new bone.

canine tooth
A pointed tooth used for grasping and piercing, also called a fang. Humans have four small canines but carnivores such as cats and dogs have long, sharp canines.

cartilage
A tough, rubbery tissue that forms the inside of the ears and nose, and makes up large parts of the skeleton in young children. A smooth, glossy kind of cartilage lines the ends of bones where they meet in a joint.

cell
A microscopic living structure that contains genes in a central nucleus, surrounded by a jellylike fluid called cytoplasm in which many chemical reactions take place. Cells make up all the body's tissues.

cochlea
A tiny spiral chamber in the inner ear that gives us the sense of hearing. The cochlea detects sound vibrations in the fluid within it and reacts by sending nerve signals to the brain.

collagen
A tough, fibrous protein found in many parts of the body, particularly bone, cartilage, and skin.

condyle
A rounded, knucklelike projection on a bone that forms part of a joint.

cranium
The part of the skull that houses the brain. The cranium is also called the braincase.

diaphragm
A sheet of muscle under the lungs that pulls flat to make the lungs suck in air during breathing.

embryo
A baby in the first eight weeks of development. After eight weeks it is called a fetus.

extension
A movement that straightens a joint. The name extensor indicates a muscle that has this action. The extensor digitorum, for instance, extends the fingers.

fertilization
The joining of an egg cell from a woman with a sperm cell from a man. The fertilized cell will develop into a baby.

fetus
An unborn baby between eight weeks after fertilization and birth.

flexion
A movement that bends a joint. The name flexor indicates a muscle that has this action. The flexor carpi ulnaris, for instance, bends the wrist.

fracture
A break in a bone. Fractures vary from fine hairline cracks to major injuries that break bones into separate fragments.

hormone
A chemical that circulates in the blood and changes the way certain parts of the body work. Growth hormone, for instance, makes bones grow longer.

incisor tooth
A tooth at the front of the mouth used for cutting and gripping food. Children have four incisors, the same number as adults.

joint
The meeting point between two or more bones. Most joints anchor the bones together but allow them to move.

lever
A simple mechanical device that pivots (swings) around a fixed point. The body's bones work as levers.

ligament
A tough fibrous band that holds two bones together. Many ligaments are flexible, but they cannot be stretched.

lumbar
Relating to the part of the body between the lowest ribs and the top of the hip bone. The lumbar vertebrae are in the lower back.

molar tooth
A tooth used for grinding and crushing.

muscle
A type of body tissue that can contract quickly when triggered by a nerve signal. Muscles attached to bones make the human body move.

nerve
A part of the body that is shaped like a cable and carries electric signals along nerve cells.

nerve signal
An electrical signal that travels along a nerve.

occipital
Relating to the back of the head. The occipital bone is the rear part of the skull.

orbit
A bowl-shaped hollow in the skull in which an eye sits. Orbits are also called eye sockets.

organ
A large body part that carries out a particular job. The heart, stomach, and brain are organs.

ossicles
Three small bones in the middle ear that transmit sound vibrations to the fluid-filled inner ear.

osteoblast
A type of cell that creates new bone tissue. Osteoblasts secrete the calcium minerals that make bones hard.

osteoclast
A type of cell that breaks down and removes bone tissue. Osteoclasts help remodel the skeleton, removing bone that isn't needed.

pelvis
The large bony frame that the leg bones connect to. The pelvis is made up of the hip bones and the bottom of the spine.

process
A part of a bone that sticks out, providing an attachment site for a ligament or tendon.

protein
A substance that serves as an important building block in many living tissues, such as muscle, skin, and bone.

puberty

The period of life when sex organs start to work, usually in the teenage years. Puberty is accompanied by a spurt in growth and various physical changes, such as breast development in girls and the deepening of the voice in boys.

sinus

An air-filled cavity in the skull. Sinuses open into the nasal cavity.

skeletal muscle

The type of muscle attached to the skeleton. Skeletal muscles are under voluntary control, but other types of muscle, such as the muscle in the heart and stomach, are involuntary.

skeleton

The framework of bones that supports and moves the body.

species

A group of organisms that are all similar and can breed with each other. Lions form a species, for example, but birds don't since there are many different species of birds.

spinal cord

A large cord of nervous tissue that runs down the middle of the spinal column, connecting the brain to the rest of the body.

suture

An immovable joint between two bones. For example, the joints between the bones that make up the braincase are sutures.

synovial joint

A movable joint, such as the knee, elbow, or shoulder. In synovial joints, the ends of the bones are covered with smooth cartilage and lubricated by a slippery liquid known as synovial fluid.

tarsal

One of the bones of the ankle.

temporal

Relating to the temples—the areas on either side of the head. The temporal bones are two bones, one on each side of the head, that form part of the cranium.

tendon

A tough, ropelike cord that attaches the end of a muscle to a bone. Tendons are also called sinews.

thoracic

To do with the thorax (chest). The thoracic vertebrae are the backbones in the chest.

thorax

The chest region, which includes the ribs, lungs, and heart.

tissue

A collection of similar cells, all of which perform one main job. Muscle, fat, nerves, and bone are all types of tissue.

vertebra

One of the bones that forms the vertebral column or backbone. The plural of vertebra is vertebrae.

X-ray

A type of light that is invisible to the human eye and can pass through soft body tissues but not through bones or teeth. Photographs taken with X-ray cameras allow doctors and dentists to see inside the body.

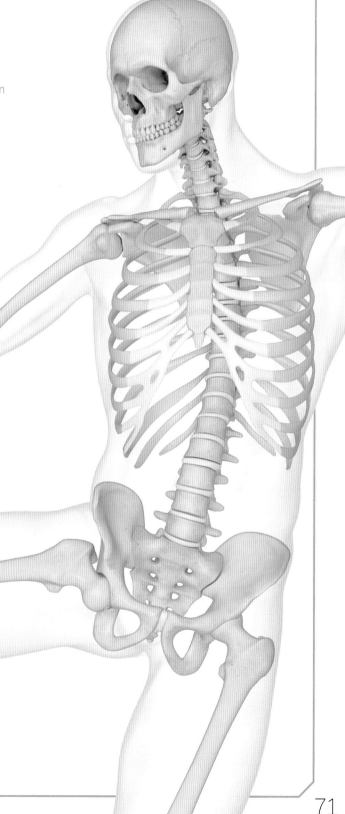

INDEX

Achilles tendon 59
amphibians 10, 38
ankles 54, 57, 59, 61
anvil 26
apes 23, 39, 54
Ardipithecus 52
arms 17, 40–41
astronauts 19
atlas 32
Australopithecus 52
axis 32
aye-aye 43

babies 14–16
babirusa 31
backbone 8, 9, 34–37, 47
balance 52, 59, 61
ball-and-socket joints 20, 21, 50
bat 11, 15, 43
bear 60
beaver 29
biceps 41
birds 10, 11, 33, 40, 47
  dove 11
  eagle 40
  hornbill 23
  ostrich 33
  owl 27
  penguin 11
  pigeon 11, 47
blood cells 12, 54
blood vessels 18, 22, 23, 31
blue whale 23
bone marrow 12, 13, 54
bones
  artificial 62–63
  broken 18–19
  development of 14–15
  fusing 16, 17
  inside 12–13
brain 22, 23, 25
  evolution of 24
braincase 24–25
breathing 46–47
bullfrog 10

calcaneus 58
calcium phosphate 12, 13, 31
callus 18–19
calves 59
canine teeth 28
carbon dating 65
carbon fiber 62, 63
carnivores 28, 29
carp 10
carpal bones 41, 42

cartilage 12, 14, 15, 16
  broken bones 18–19
  joints 21, 50
cerebellum 25
cervical vertebrae 34
cheetah 37
chest 46–47
chewing 28
chimpanzee 33, 45, 54
clavicle 17, 38
coccyx 34, 35, 36
cochlea 26
collagen 13
collarbone 17, 38
compact bone 12, 19
condyloid joints 21, 59
cow 49
cranium 22, 32
crocodile 15, 31
crowns, teeth 29, 30
CT (computer tomography)
  scanners 63

deer 11
dentine 31
diaphragm 46
digitigrade animals 60
disks, spinal 36, 37
DNA 65
dog 33
dolphin 11, 40
dove 11

eagle 40
ears 26, 27
eggs 15
Egyptians, ancient 64–65
elbow 20, 21, 40, 41
elephant 31, 51
enamel 31
endoskeleton 9
epiphyseal plates 17
evolution 10–11, 33, 52
exoskeletons 9, 62
eyes 27
eye socket 23, 27

face 26
  reconstruction 65
false ribs 46
feet 58–61
femur 51, 53, 54–55
fibula 53
field of view 27
fingers 14, 42–45
fish 10, 38
flippers 40
floating ribs 46

foramen magnum 22, 33
forensic science 65
fossils 65
fractures 18–19
frog 10
funny bone 40
gibbon 11, 39
giraffe 29, 32, 33
gorilla 9, 49, 60
growth plates 17
guinea pig 11

hammer 26
hamstrings 57
hands 17, 42–43
  bionic 62–63
  hard callus 19
head
  turning 20, 32
  see also skull
hearing 26, 27
heart 47
heels 58, 59, 61
herbivores 28, 29
hinge joints 21
hips 20, 34, 48–49, 54
  artificial 51
  joints 50–51
Homo erectus 52
Homo habilis 65
hoofed mammals 11, 49, 60
hornbill 23
horse 47, 60
howler monkey 33
humerus 19, 38, 40
hyoid bone 33

iguana 51
ilium bone 49
incisors 28, 29
ischium 48, 49

jaws 22, 28–29
jellyfish 9
joints
  elbow 21
  fingers and thumbs 9, 42, 44
  hip 50–51
  knee 21, 54, 56–57
  and movement 8, 9, 20–21
  neck 20, 32
  shoulder 20, 38–39
  spinal 37
  types of 21

kangaroo 11, 58
knees

joint 21, 54, 56–57
  kneecap 15, 56
knuckles 9, 21
koala 45

legs 17, 52–53
  evolution of 10, 38
ligaments 8, 43, 49, 50, 56, 57
lion 29
liquid skeletons 9
lizards 10, 23, 47, 58
lumbar vertebrae 34
lungs 46–47

mammals 11, 51
marsupials 11
masseter muscle 28
maxilla 29
metacarpals 42
metal plates 18
metatarsals 58, 61
milk teeth 30, 31
molars 28, 29
mole 40
monkeys 23, 39
  howler monkey 33
  rhesus monkey 39
  spider monkey 23, 35, 45
mouse 55
mouth 28–29
movement 9, 20–21
MRI (magnetic resonance imaging) scanners 63
mummification 64–65
muscles
  biting and chewing 28
  contraction 8, 9
  running and walking 57
  skeletal 9

nails 45
narwhal 31
Neanderthals 24
neck bones 20, 32–33, 34
nerves 22, 23, 25, 31, 34
newt 10
nose 26, 27
nuchal ligament 32

olfactory receptors 26
opposable thumbs 44, 45
opposable toes 60
Oreopithecus 52
ossicles 15
osteoblasts 19
osteoclasts 19
ostrich 33, 58
owl 27

patella 56
pelvis 16, 48–49
penguin 11
phalanges 58, 59, 61
pigeon 11, 47
pivot joints 21
plane joints 21
plantigrade animals 60
polar bear 27
premolars 28, 29
primates 11
prosthetics 62–63
puberty 49
pubis 49
python 37

quadriceps 57

radius 41
rat 15
reptiles 10, 23, 51
rhesus monkey 39
rhinoceros 55
ribs/rib cage 8, 20, 34, 46–47
rodents 11
running 51, 52–53, 57

sacrum 34, 48
saddle joints 21
salamander 10
scanning machines 63
scapula 38
scorpion 9
seal, elephant 47
sense organs 22, 23, 26–27
shark 10, 31
sheep, bighorn 23
shoulder blades 38
shoulder joints 20, 38–39
shrew, hero 37
sinuses 24
skeletal muscles 9
skull 9, 22–23
  animals 23
  babies 14
  growth of 16–17
  inside 24–25
sloth 43
smell, sense of 26, 27
snake 10, 29, 37
soft callus 18
sperm whale 49
spider monkey 23, 35, 45
spinal column 34–35, 47
  flexibility 36–37
spinal cord 25, 32, 34, 36
spongy bone 12, 19, 54
sternum 46, 47

stirrup 26
stomach 47
support 8
synovial fluid 21

tailbone 34, 35
tails 35
tarsals 59, 61
tarsier 27, 43
teeth 28–29
  growing 30–31
temporal bone 22, 27
temporal muscle 28
tendons 8, 43, 56, 57
  Achilles tendon 59
thighbone 12–13, 54–55
thoracic vertebrae 34
thumbs 44–45
tibia 53, 56
titanosaurs 55
toad 10
toes 14, 58, 59, 60–61
tortoise 10
true ribs 46
turbinate bones 26, 27
turtle 10, 47
Tyrannosaurus 35

ulna 41
unguligrade animals 60

vertebrae 8
  neck 32
  spinal column 34–37
vertebrates 9, 10–11
  development of 15
viper 29
vision 27

Wadlow, Robert 16
walking 57
  feet 58, 60, 61
  hip joints 51
  upright 52, 54
whale 11, 23, 40, 49
wings 40
wolf 39, 60
woven bone 19
wrist 21, 41

X-ray 63

ACKNOWLEDGMENTS
Dorling Kindersley would like to thank Steve Crozier for photo retouching, Nic Dean for picture research, Christine Heilman for Americanization, Sarah MacLeod for editorial assistance, and Helen Peters for the index.
The publisher would like to thank the following for their kind permission to reproduce their photographs:
(Key: a-above; b-below/bottom; c-centre; f-far; l-left; r-right; t-top)
9 123RF.com: reddz (br). **Dorling Kindersley**: Linda Pitkin (bc). **10 Dorling Kindersley**: Geoff Brightling / Booth Museum of Natural History, Brighton (cr); Colin Keates / Natural History Museum, London (br). **11 Alamy Stock Photo**: Iakov Filimonov (cl). **Dorling Kindersley**: Andy Crawford / Courtesy of the Natural History Museum, London (br); Steve Gorton / Courtesy of Oxford Univeristy Museum of Natural History (tc); Alex Wilson / Booth Museum of Natural History, Brighton (cr). **Getty Images**: Les Stocker (clb/Barking deer). **12 Science Photo Library**: Steve Gschmeissner (tc); Susumu Nishinaga (tl). **15 Science Photo Library**: James Hanken (tr); Microscape (cr); Paul Tafforeau (ESRF)/La

Ferme aux Crocodiles de Pierrelatte (br). **16 Getty Images**: Bettmann (bl). **Science Photo Library**: Microscape (tr). **17 Science Photo Library**: (growing hands). **19 NASA** (crb). **Science Photo Library**: Steve Gschmeissner (cr). **23 naturepl.com**: Neil Lucas (tr). **touchpress.com** (cra). **24 Alamy Stock Photo**: klovenbach (bl). **27 Corbis**: Matton Collection / Torb rn Arvidson (br); Matthias Breiter / Minden Pictures (c/Polar bear). **Dreamstime.com**: Olga Khoroshunova (tr). **29 Alamy Stock Photo**: The Natural History Museum (giraffe). **Photoshot**: NHPA (Gaboon viper). **touchpress.com** (lion, beaver). **31 © Bone Clones, boneclones.com** (br/Babirusa). **Jean-Christophe Theil** (crb/Mako shark skull). **43 Alamy Stock Photo**: RGB Ventures (cra); Rosanne Tackberry (crb). **Dorling Kindersley**: Rollin Verlinde (cr). **naturepl.com**: David Tipling (br). **45 123RF.com**: vincentstthomas (fcra). **Alamy Stock Photo**: epa european pressphoto agency b v (fcr). **Corbis**: DLILLC (cra). **naturepl.com**: Jouan & Rius (br). **Photoshot**: Mint Images (cr). **Science Photo Library**: Gerry Pearce (fbr). **50 Dorling Kindersley**: Geoff Dann / Courtesy of SOMSO (cl). **51 123RF**.

com: Jonathan Pledger (br). **Corbis**: Westend 61 GmbH (crb). **Science Photo Library**: Lawrence Livermore National Labatory (c). **56 Alamy Stock Photo**: Wavebreak Media Ltd (br). **58 Alamy Stock Photo**: Gallo Images (bl). **Corbis**: Frans Lanting (cl). **Getty Images**: Renaud Visage (fbl). **naturepl.com**: Bence Mate (clb). **60 Alamy Stock Photo**: blickwinkel (bc). **61 Alamy Stock Photo**: RosalreneBetancourt (tr). **62 Courtesy of Ekso Bionics** (bl). **Touch Bionics** (c/bionic hand). **63 Dreamstime.com**: Mikhail Druzhinin (bl). **Getty Images**: Bloomberg / Chris Ratcliffe (br); BSIP / UIG (br). **Science Photo Library**: James King-Holmes (tr). **Touch Bionics** (tl). **64 Alamy Stock Photo**: Edwin Baker (tr). **64-65 The Trustees of the British Museum** (c). **65 Corbis**: Blue Jean Images (br). **Dorling Kindersley**: Colin Keates / Natural History Museum, London (c). **Kennis & Kennis / Alfons and Adrie Kennis** (tc/Homo habilis reconstruction). **Science Photo Library**: Volker Steger (cr)
All other images © Dorling Kindersley
For further information see: www.dkimages.com

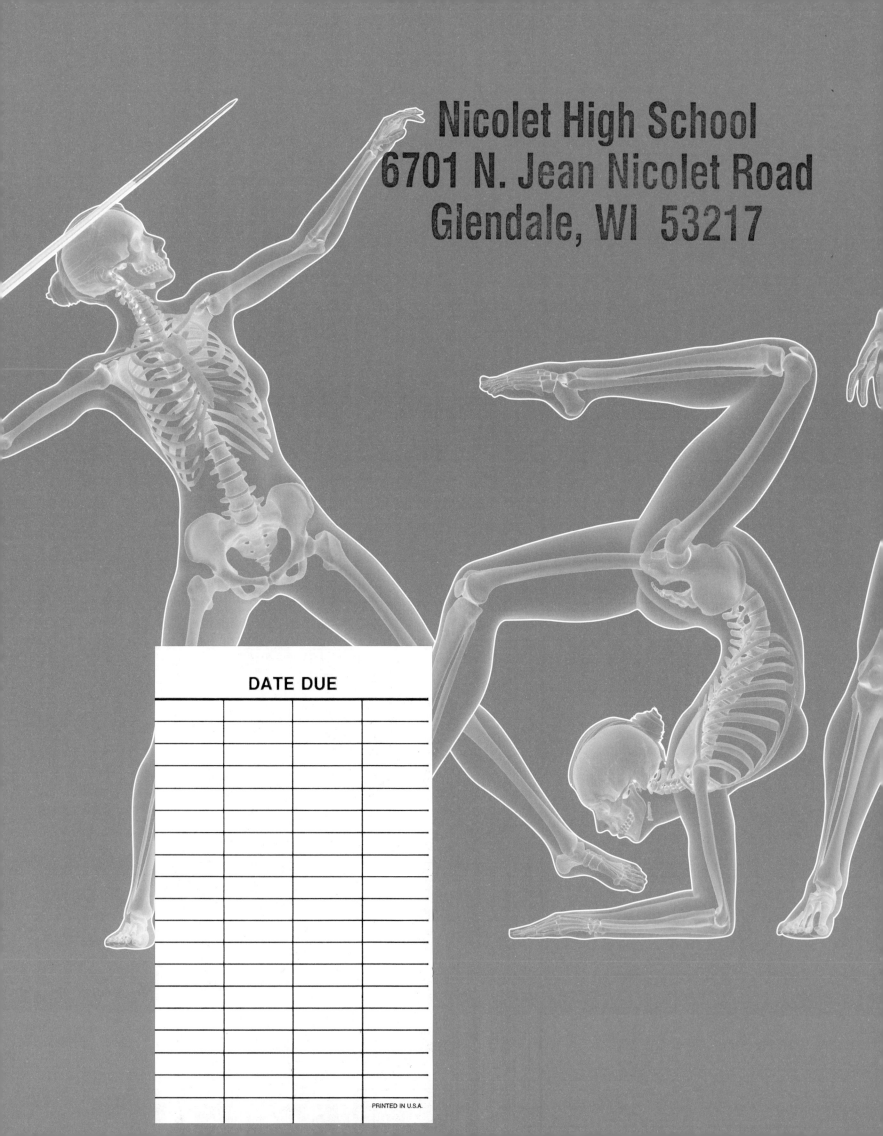

Nicolet High School
6701 N. Jean Nicolet Road
Glendale, WI 53217

DATE DUE

PRINTED IN U.S.A.